The Little Death of Self

Marianne Boruch

The Little Death of Self

NINE ESSAYS TOWARD POETRY

UNIVERSITY OF MICHIGAN PRESS

Ann Arbor

Published in the United States of America by the
University of Michigan Press
Manufactured in the United States of America
♾ Printed on acid-free paper

2020   2019   2018   2017   4   3   2   1

A CIP catalog record for this book is available from the British Library.

Library of Congress Cataloging-in-Publication data has been applied for.

ISBN: 978-0-472-07347-4 [hardcover]
ISBN: 978-0-472-05347-6 [paper]
ISBN: 978-0-472-12277-6 [ebook]

I do not care for "systems," what concerns me is the philosophy of the astonished.

—George Oppen

Contents

To Warn and to Acknowledge

A broken record it's called, my family's favorite complaint about sitting too long in one place, listening to whatever and whomever. And one dreams off in self-defense. But writing poems—or essays, for that matter–is stranger than that, the needle skipping on an old turntable to a most interior ache. Which is to say, the line between poetry (the delicate, surprising not-quite) and the essay (the emphatic what-about) is thin, easily crossed. And I'm fond of the leap.

After all, unlike fiction these two genres work beyond a human sense of time. Each welcomes deep meditation, each hopelessly mixes image and idea and runs with scissors, each resists asking for directions at the gas station, each can distrust the notion of premise or formulaic progression. As for these essays in particular, they started out in dusk or daylight, many by way of a curious detail or question that would not quit—i.e., how are poems like airplanes, unbelievably heavy but light enough to fly? Or just how does hunger work on the brain, on what the eye is able finally to understand as image in some crucial middle distance that draws us into the great world?

Quite a lot of this book called for my loitering in fields of expertise about which I knew little, then some, then perhaps enough through my reading and observation and conversations with thoughtful people to be forgiven my delving into aviation, music, anatomy, history, medicine, photography, fiction, neuroscience, physics, anthropology, painting, and drawing. It's that I'm addicted to metaphor, the love between unlike things, and *only connect*—I tend to believe E. M. Forster on this. Now and then I repeat ideas, references to writers, what they said or wrote. Such moments are refrains of a sort, *inter-essay* affection at work, irrepressible admiration which bears repeating. Keats, Stevens, Frost, Plath, Auden, Bishop, and others: I like to imagine they're haunting me, but I suspect I'm the one stalking them.

Everything here began as lectures, mostly for the Warren Wilson College Program for Writers, and but also for Purdue University, the University of Edinburgh, the Bread Loaf Writers' Conference, and Georgia College's Center for Studies in Flannery O'Connor. All came—the most inward painstaking *doing* of them—the same mysterious way poems arrive, through image and anecdote into lyric time via pools and eddies and weird long stretches that surprised and allowed me in, to what I hadn't first imagined. As with poems, a lot of silence was involved, a lot of staring into the page and into space. I mainly wanted to return seriously to poets whose work I love, mull over the fact that writing and reading poetry alters us, that there is no *us* really, just the *I/thou* and stopped time when we pay close attention. And then we look back to a changed world.

Many thanks to friends, colleagues, students, or conference participants who heard one or more of these essays as lectures or read them later and spoke with me about them, and to those editors of journals who first ran these pieces, sometimes in a slightly different form: *New England Review* ("The End inside It" and "Diagnosis, Poetry, and the Burden of Mystery"); *American Poetry Review* ("The Little Death of Self," "Three Blakes," and "Heavy Lifting"); *The Georgia Review* ("Is and Was," and "O'Connor plus Bishop plus Closely plus Distance"); and *Massachusetts Review* ("Seeing Things" and "Charm). "The End Inside It," and "Heavy Lifting" were republished online via *Poetry Daily.* And "Three Blakes" has been included in *William Blake: Bloom's Modern Critical Views* (New York: Chelsea House, 2016). Special thanks to Kathleen Shoemaker, Librarian of the Rose Manuscript, Archives & Rare Book Library at Emory University, for aiding and abetting my use of Elizabeth Bishop's letters to Flannery O'Connor, first made available in 2016, well after I wrote the earlier version of "O'Connor plus Bishop plus Closely plus Distance." The version included here reflects both sides of that fascinating correspondence.Warm thoughts to linguists Mary Niepokuj and April Ginther for information about verb tense and the scientific method, to painter Matilda Hungerford for her ideas about perspective, to Elizabeth Adcock for introducing me to the work of Adrien Stoutenberg, and to Brooks Haxton for reminding me of Sidney's "Astrophel and Stella" behind Larkin's poem "Sad Steps."

And loving gratitude to David Dunlap, sounding board first and last, generous reader of all drafts, and to Will Dunlap, especially for his musical advice which aided a number of these pieces, and for his man-at-the-window story that helped me think toward the essay "Is and Was."

My gratitude to the Fulbright Foundation, the University of Edinburgh and its Institute for the Advanced Study in the Humanities, and Purdue, for the support for my six months of research in the UK as I prepared for the Conan Doyle/Keats essay.

Finally, this book is for Margaret Moan Rowe, and in memory of Bill Keirce, wry and rare spirits.

The End Inside It

On the radio, Merce said, *Do it,*
Jump first, then run,
even when it was just with his arms, when he got old,
even if some people hated it.
    —Jean Valentine, from *Break the Glass*

Or *closure*, as it's called among poets but not a "we need closure on this" sort of thing, certainly not that cheap and cheesy "because we have to get on with our lives" though at the end of all poems is the return to the day as it was, its noon light or later, supper and whatever madness long over, reading in bed those few minutes, next to the little table lamp. But to come out of the poem's tunnel of words—the best way is to be blinking slightly, released from some dark, eyes adjusting, what was ordinary seen differently now. Or not. At times the shift from reading to not reading is so graceful it's transparent, the poem itself Robert Frost's "piece of glass" skimmed from winter's icy drinking trough and held up to melt and melt the real world into real dream, then back, his moment of clarity unto mystery returned to clarity again. Of course, that actual gesture comes early in his "After Apple Picking," a poem full of what might "trouble" his dreams in the wake of such hard work. Its last line is one low-key gulp, his "Or just some human sleep" itself following something about exhaustion more wistful and weird: "Were he not gone, / The woodchuck could say whether it was like his / Long sleep, as I describe its coming on." As in—hey! Let's ask this woodchuck here, shall we? And how absolutely odd and brilliant that we never see this move as comic, though it could be right out of Bugs Bunny or Bart Simpson, depending on when you started to find things funny. But Frost isn't funny, at least not in this poem where sleep isn't exactly sleep either.

Such sleight-of-hand only proves how tone can control things in poems and that success, if not triumph, is largely in the accumulation of word, syntax, cadence tangled and guided by two seemingly warring elements—fever and tact, right to the end. Plus how unexpectedly but inevitably any final moment emerges out of all that has gone before, the rise and fall, the order of those choices as they press a wayward, fierce descent down the page or in the air to make the poem *mean*. Frost wrote this too: "Theme alone can steady us down." And maybe he's right, though we don't much use that t-word anymore.

I love what Marianne Moore left behind in an essay: "I tend to like a poem which instead of culminating in a crescendo, merely comes to a close." Note well her "merely"—one of the many things in Moore to put on pause and willfully distrust. But her remark suggests at least two kinds of ending: the grand orchestration vs. the simple *okay*—shrug—*it's over.* Frost's "Or just some human sleep" lies clearly in this second category, though something remains vulnerable and lasting in that sound. The choices here—the poet's *or*, his *just*, his *some*, all together now: his "or just some human sleep"—conspire to a studied indifference, an *almost* indifference in spite of that wide-eyed "human" there. More, that "human" up against a woodchuck's apparent untroubled sleep makes sudden and eerie how unknowable we ourselves are. News flash: words *mean* things. And *human* here at the bottom of all that comes earlier, its underscored double beat cast among this small run of single stressed words is, no, not a crescendo. Moore would approve, I think, if what anyone thinks might matter to her now that she's past any ending, though of course one could argue she isn't. Her poems, at least, are not. They *keep* ending. Which is yet another crucial thing about poetic closure.

Whatever Moore's fondness for no trumpeting as a poem slips back into silence, her own endings carry a range of findings. I say "findings" since she refused to call them poems at all but "exercises in composition," though that may be like saying good doctors only "practice" medicine when the patient, recovering against all odds, proves something more serious going on. Three findings then, although admittedly pulled out of context—which must be illegal, this marking the branch and not the whole tree.

First: from possibly her most anthologized poem, "The Fish," the final two sentences threaded down through four uneven lines do what seems to have pleased this poet most, lay out a genuinely abstract statement: "Repeated / evidence has proved that it can live / on what can not revive / its youth." (puzzling, that, as only Moore can puzzle), followed by the visible, the charged. "The sea grows old in it," she wrote, as if this were afterthought, a fresh discovery, and yet, Moore being Moore, bewildering too, despite the hard beauty of the ocean's expanse.

That we reach the mind's eye through sound makes the process here quite physical: rambling, then abrupt, a distant, busy, abstraction-laden sentence pulled up short by a final one of six single stresses, three and three, perfectly balanced, relatively clear but baffling all the same, especially that final note: "grows old in it." You can feel the jolt in your body, so yes, it must be true! She's that alert, even to the tiniest of words! *In it*. When has the word "in" ever had such power? You can mull and mull this a long time until the whole notion of fish, of time, of watery depths quite overwhelms. Then again, Moore's obsession was both to stay and shift, to think and finally abandon that thinking, so, too bad, she might have said about any second-guessing, *too bad*. And then: *I have other "exercises" to write.*

For instance, take her poem "Propriety" and its ending, far more chatty, even arch, but it too keeps turning and comes to rest past wit, in an equally sobering and mysterious light—not to mention how along the way she reinvents the pansy as a sidenote, taking everything cute and squishy out of it:

> Brahms and Bach,
> no; Bach and Brahms. To thank Bach
> for his song
> first, is wrong.
> Pardon me;
> both are the
> unintentional pansy-face
> uncursed by self-inspection; blackened
> because born that way.

A final example is her "Nevertheless"; its last four lines pose a question, then a second one, which alchemizes to exclamation: "What is there / like fortitude?" Moore asks. "What sap / went through that little thread / to make the cherry red!" Abstract statement—whose ante is upped to way-more-direct and welcoming by its syntactical delivery as question—becomes image again. It's simile now, metaphorical, which makes it half and half, abstraction and the real thing too—we've all seen a cherry, we know that sweet drill—but this poet's observant fascination with the natural world is quirky, an imagining down to a near-molecular level.

Clearly Moore is one smart cookie, and the sound of thinking is a thing we might relish, closing our eyes to call her poems back in some dark room of remembering. It's a double whammy; she *thinks* about her thinking—which almost overdoes its grown-up job as elevated assertion, though her whimsy is a counterforce, a kind of hesitation that keeps each poem considering its options even as it decidedly bows out.

I end, you end, we all end—sure, okay. And we mime that cruel or solacing fact in poems, hoping for something both sensible and strange, assuming that's a preferred outcome. Take this, says the doctor, and his reckoning is drift or delusion through all hollows and impassable places, however they layer. The poem tangles or it weaves. Either way, careful. We make that.

One of the simple, great things about poems is that for the most part they are small inventions—a page, two pages. That is, we can be there with them; we can hover, literally over them, a few moments for the eye, an ear to them briefly, and how many breaths from first line to last? Not that many. Which is to say, in reading—as *reader*—the finished thing or in its morphing into revision if we're actually the *writer thereof*, we can enter into it again and again until all becomes a kind of soothsaying in reverse, to stare at a poem (as reader) or its draft (as writer) and note how the ending in fact comes to be, came to be, or could come to be, bringing its most secret life as both earned thing—fashionable to say "earned" now—and as deep surprise. (See Frost, via one of his old chestnuts, his "no surprise in the writer, no surprise in the reader." And who doesn't love that easier-said-than-done rule?) But there must be a map somewhere, however dim, a trail that ends in the Minotaur's cave. Perhaps reason, if not willful cause, can be gleaned, a trigger for the poem's closure-to-be if not a full body press running from start to finish.

So consider something as commonly shocking as a dissection lab, medical school, where what little backstory the students get on their cadavers includes gender (though it's obvious) and age (not that clear) and cause of death (rarely immediately apparent). The body opens like a gift or like a shipwrecked trunk full of treasure, however waterlogged, splintered by rocks, locks busted, hinges sprung. So one peers *into* these fellow creatures for weeks, into a him, a her, whoever they were, they *are*. And one finds clues way back—that's what the mind is programmed to do. One begins to notice what it was that led forward to this moment beyond death, to these shiny tables in this glaring light. It doesn't take much of a prophet to say: lungs filled to the brim with bad yogurt-esque stuff equals pneumonia, or that plaque so thick in the aorta means *the heart just stopped*. More intricate might be those tiny pouches springing off the colon like so many puddle-colored Christmas tree lights—diverticulitis in the oldest cadaver, say (but she had years and years, so there!), or the liver in the big guy, ominously speckled. To those still breathing, to you or to me, such things suggest a future, *be warned*, a cautionary tale to those of us left behind in the world. To the dead: it's the past, fable and illustration and proof. They've months ago boarded that boat to the afterlife by lantern light in some Doré-like etching and now we stand above them to track and figure. With pattern comes clarity, the future by way of the past seems inevitable, bad news that pressed forward as an inescapable given, though one hopes for amazement which amounts, in fact, to a timeless *staring into*, however cut short by *this once*.

Is the poem a body? Underscore an honorable *yes*, and the poem keeps living. I swear it does, even after years on the page, sitting steely, all knowing enough, *selected* or *collected* or *anthologized*, its maker decades under the sod. Miss Moore? Her rush to get to that blinding red cherry and its fortitude before checking out altogether in her poem "Nevertheless" is egged on and engineered by her sharp-eyed detail from the very start, the body of her poem taking up the natural world in such bursts of appreciative wonder that the tercets she makes barely do the trick of holding all in order as her semi-manic, stop/start enjambment pushes forward. How calmly she takes off, but how haywire things get. "Nevertheless" is, in fact, her title and first word, starting the piece in mid-argument; then she steps sideways. So— "nevertheless"

> you've seen a strawberry
> that's had a struggle; yet
> was, where the fragments met,
>
> a hedgehog or a star-
> fish for the multitude
> of seeds.

To go on by way of Moore's raised, peculiar eyebrow is to find some saving grace in rubber tree roots that "still grow / in frozen ground," this "once where / there was a prickly-pear- / leaf clinging to barbed wire," then those carrots stunted—grown big as a "mandrakes / or a ram's horn root some- / times." But it's the grape tendril that incites real awe, as it

> ties a knot in knots till
>
> knotted thirty times,—so
> the bound twig that's under-
> gone and over-gone, can't stir.

All these details loom up and recede like something out of dream as we fall from line to line, larger to smaller to larger again, as the poem makes the experience of looking at such things quite alive for us, the dreamer so meticulous in her mapping. If this poem *were* a body, we'd see a series of small wrong-ways, little crash-and-burns battled by muscle and vessel foreshadowing a final resistance that no, won't work forever— but now, what a fight! (The nerve of the real nerve, say, that takes over for a defunct nearby one in the leg, or the lung which works double time when the other one deflates forever.) Partly it's Moore's shrewd plain connectives that acknowledge defeat and buck up regardless: her "yet," her "still," her "once." Then it's her blurting out "Victory won't come / to me unless I go to it." Her qualifying *unless* reads as human hope, just a thread of it, before her musing on those hyperactive, resilient grape tendrils kicks in. The rhymes in the poem—her "till" and "tendril" and "where" and "there" earlier, her "yet" and "met"—could be other attempts to make things all right even as her emphatic, surprising enjambment stands apart, well, amused.

The body doesn't work or it does, or it doesn't, or it. . . . Moore's counterpoint is a kind of breathing, reminding me of another one of Frost's claims, that "there is no advance, only expansion and contraction." Finally this poem is poised to end in the astonishment suggested all along by shifts of scale, then her line breaks' fractured words and double-dealing which, in turn, imply control, a certain distance. Distance enough, I think, to make her choice of near-aphorism credible again, for—and in spite of—how universally inward and thus inarguable it seems, her noting how "The weak overcomes / its menace, the strong over- / comes itself," dipping into—God forbid—what we might cliché as "a teachable moment." Yet not for long, because Moore really isn't a moralist but loves the world instead—her real saving grace—finally ending in image and its flash of life. Besides, she's way too weird. After what's come before, this ending is loud, fully voiced, a question, an exclamation in motion as if we're out of dream now, stunned into the blinking realization I've mentioned before: "What is there / like fortitude?" she nearly, then really, shouts: "What sap / went through that little thread / to make the cherry red!"

Happiness? So is this an ode of sorts, to *that?* But there's dark in those knots, the "bound twig," her smited-unto-epic carrots. Moore was a hard-ass, never Pollyanna. She makes trouble—not misery—with her twisted imagery and her enjambment off its pins, on edge.

It occurs to me to add that as I write this, I hear things. Downstairs, a new sound, really an old sound at the door, *key in,* a low pure pitch, no duration to speak of, then another sound as the key turns. I hear it, its teeth fit, or maybe I hear this since I know a key has teeth—or has been bitten itself to have them. I picture the small wheeze, the push to unlock. And the pleasure—*he's home*, which is to say, *we're both home*—at the hinge sound, the sound of the door-as-it-opens sound, a slight drag to it, its weight lifted, part of it doesn't want to. But that rush of air anyway, outside to inside, a stop, a giving up, to go on.

That *stop*—an unsettling, engaging impulse as poems zero down to meet their end. I thought this largely due to a hit of dissonance, a musical idea with a long history and still affecting what resolution—another loved term—means to composers, at least. And of course, there's a heart-stopping angle in that major to minor key business. But dissonance: never the nice dinner party, always the unstable move. In music, it could mean one note set uncomfortably close to another and the ear resists, a seeming misstep, pain in that, though exciting in small doses until it's all begging for consonance—a little room, please—a return to something balanced, bearable, the space between notes familiar, and if not particularly happy, that moment, at least gracefully unhappy. Consonance as "a point of arrival," says Roger Kamein, reigning archduke of music theory, "of rest, of resolution." This may be one of the simplest definitions of beauty: you build anyway—it could hurt—then you release.

About poetry, we don't exactly say dissonance, though *tension* makes the point, or *contrast*: force stopped by a counterforce, a yes, a no, then perhaps beyond that somewhere. And required— here's Frost again—his surprise as a key outcome to any twisting of thought into afterthought. For instance, there's the long rambling soliloquy that makes up the bulk of the poem "Chinese Leftovers" by Mark Halliday, where the anxious, witty, by turns self-aggrandizing and self-deprecating speaker laments his life. In short, he's lonely and alone ("Oh lord, once / on this sofa I wrote truly poignant lines about Cathy!"); he's read himself into a stupor, great book after great book ("When I think of the hours— / . . . lost dozing over *Felix Holt*"); he's at odds with his old dad ("maybe *you* would be the right son for my father"). So he's tipped back a couple of beers and actually written those words down—"two Budweisers at midnight"—as a thing to do, that he's done. Now what? What *can* happen out of a messy outburst this funny and whiny and earnest? The turn, sonnet-like, is quiet, almost sweetly to the point. "I'm sort of in trouble," the speaker tells no one, the register all at once lowered. It's like something patched through on a bad radio. And in the treasured tradition of the lyric, as Auden saw it, we lean in to *overhear* this private realization, and sink with it too. A couple of choices here, unto proverb: we can laugh or we can weep. And either could mean empathy. Still, how Halliday pulls away from all the earlier whirling that caused this more internal admission is thrilling. And why not? *I'm sort of in trouble.* Partly—that's all of us, right? Its dark lift, regardless, must be part chemical, natural opiates in the brain, I'm told, released whenever a thing clicks and resolves.

So many ways to do this—to write a poem's last words. Options, then, even as endings must grow out of all that comes before. Most are self-inflicted; others just aren't, at least not entirely. The fact is we hear poetic closure quite differently over time. It can depend on literary fashion, breathed in like air. We can't help it. What's cool or, more to the point, what's not cool, could mean an ending once okay enough, now seeming tedious, *so yesterday*—the horror, the horror—melodrama slipping in and you read it over and over to diagnose: too willful or plain pretentious, too breathless, veering toward precious, too big bang beautiful for this ironic age, too *something*. Or the kind of closure we'll even consider as we dream up and revise becomes a matter of where we are in our reading or writing lives, or that we've changed by way of a lived perspective: had children or car wrecks, watched too many die, gotten married or unmarried or hopelessly transfixed by a very pretty river. It could be simply how much patience we have, or what we want more of at the end: danger or safety, a new planet or a scene close to where we started, though there are other depths to fathom, beyond such a dichotomy. We're sometimes told there's a greater plan. In my first time as a child, say, maybe end rhyme was solace against all things unnerving but only if I believe the classic assumption, that to be a kid is to be adrift in strangeness and the young self needs grounding to feel safe. In its repeat repeat, rhyme does that handily. A reasonable theory, but honestly, I don't recall that particular delight as rescue, a shading that strikes me now as rather adult, a gravity after the fact. Anyway, sometimes a child, blessedly burdened with a watchful, heart-in-the-mouth mother, yearns and burns to be scared, to slip, to escape her loving eye.

Still, the sonnet's finale—at least Shakespeare's two-tone click-shut version, that calm couplet sound earned by the usual knock-down drag-out of its twelve-line argument—did set a precedent in the sixteenth century for the poem as thought device, poetry *in motion*, a finally-figuring-out to a last *ta-da!* or *duh!* or just a low-note *yes*, coming after. When it's windy and really dark in the mind, not much can beat the charm of a couplet. "For thy sweet love remembered such wealth brings / That then I scorn to change my state with kings"—so ends Shakespeare's famous #29 after much ado about envy and "disgrace with fortune and men's eyes" and other personal disasters. The ghost of the sonnet is all over free verse too, including that two-step feel of closure, this essay's epigraph from Jean Valentine's poem "I dropped a Plate" for example, the complication and comfort in the couplet-like ring of her ending lines as she invites in Merce Cunningham at ninety, still dancing: "even when it was just his arms, when he got old / even if some people hated it." And there, the singing same thing comes first in each line, her *even*, and her *even* again.

Shakespeare's last twinning lines that rhyme their end-stop words—first "brings," then "kings"—do *mean* in a large rhetorical way, his sonnet's shining thread gone public in the ore. Two threads, though, two lines, add up to relief most emphatically, a sort of literary equivalent to what musicians call the "amen cadence" to finish off a piece, a "remote distance" kind of gathering-up we might remember from church, sung out—*a-men*—the "a" and "men" so much the same really, just a few notes' difference and like siblings who look alike, born a couple of years apart, holding hands, jumping triumphant off the roof together (though one hopes for a trampoline below). As that musical cadence descends, a slow dark in the falling *a-men*, we hold tight to the familiar sound still floating with us, and so come home with it. And to it.

But *cadence* is a curious word, one that carries a slightly different sense in music, and not the poet's meaning, which isn't necessarily the end of anything but the rather freelance rush of *part*, not whole, of phrase on phrase to make line and sentence in any poem—the meter of that, how it sounds in the mouth and the air, all the teeth marks still on it to start and continue, winnowing pause by way of line break and comma and dash. It could end somewhere, whatever run, at any point in the poem. In music, the word "cadence" is straight out darker, referring exclusively to how things close, the end of a phrase or of individual movements—or the end of the entire business, what poets call closure—but almost always a descent, the musical cadence taking its juice from Latin, true to its originating *caditia*, "a falling from," through Italian and into Middle English still falling, all that time. Further, whether song or symphony, it's traditionally a progression of chords moving to a harmonic point of rest—the tonic—a place where things do resolve, a vivid, very physical way of expectation played out to its reward most literally. My cellist son, Will Dunlap, seemed puzzled at first by the poets' looser understanding, then turned insistent, speaking up for musicians. It *closes*, Will told me, be it a riff or the whole piece: *cadence*, end of story, whether it's large or small. And I guess that could translate into a dark life lesson: *suck it up; live with it; bit by bit or finally all at once, we all go down.* Musicians and poets include "modulation of voice" in their takes on this, voice being crucial to both, a purely human sound.

Back to Mark Halliday: his tone changing makes his "I'm sort of in trouble" as much blood and bone as any bodily gesture when his poem checks out, a credible sound in the four single stresses—*I'm/sort/of/in*—which gather to stall movement. The repetition of those single beats, in turn, force something hypnotic and inner-worldly, "a voiced pause," critic Harvey Gross has written somewhere, his notion that most repetition does a silencing trick, a fiddling with the mute button. All this, before the last word—*trouble*—kicks in as a double syllable hit, the heaviest stress first, a pure trochaic reprieve which may not fix everything as the truly nice-dinner-party iambic could with its press on the last syllable, but it does ground us, taking any reader down and down, a shade ironic in the ending upbeat, releasing nonetheless. My son is right. And this particular cadence *is* rest—it closes—how that feels after the exhausting tirade before it, to keep fragmenting and never quite dissolve, though not much more can be said, at least out loud. That's the private sound in this most private of genres, poetry, which mimes best our getting lost, being lost, and maybe, with luck, something after that. Though similar to the sonnet's ending couplet in that both are pushed inevitably by the touch-and-go adding up of argument in earlier lines, Halliday's closure is not as clearly intact or confident as what end rhyme—Shakespeare's or anyone else's—can imply. The good news? Trouble=broken=it keeps going, into aftersound.

Call it *aftersound* then. What a flood of aftersound in any decent poem! Which must be like shadow, though it doesn't walk after you but absorbs everything that went before. A living part of closure, then, not a mute postscript. Think first of the silence *before* anything as equally palpable—before the first notes of the oboe which lead into a rich welter of violins, the sound of our settling into seats, of stop-talking, of stop-thinking-those-other-thoughts. Like the sound of winter mornings, no birds but a crow or two. Or the silence of snow there, how that covers, not quite a shroud in bright air. Jump to the aftersound then—after the last crazed pooling of cymbal and French horn and clarinet have welled up and over; after what he said, what she said; after the cat's wailing out there, the car roaring off, the pavement's ice shining under the street lamp. Think actual light, the so-called "magic hour" that many filmmakers cherish, the sun gone down but you can still see everything, the intensity lost, the dark of trees abstracted, less contrast then, more merging so late in the day, more blue which is said to warm all color suddenly though it doesn't have to be sudden, the word *illumination.*

For some poets this *is* poetry, a feel for the end of things from the start; some think almost entirely in this light. Jane Kenyon, for one, did that, her poems typically honed up around simple images of days lost to walking the dog, fixing supper, driving to town, common turns of a life lived. Beloved particulars—the images—do most of the work, as in her "Evening at a Country Inn," where the speaker worries mostly about the "you" in the poem who "laughed only once all day," who might be "thinking of the accident— / of picking the slivered glass from his hair." After closely watching, then spreading before us the details of the place and the testimony of her senses—savory smells from the kitchen, "red-faced skiers" stamping in with their "Homeric" hunger, the "you" who paces and smokes—the speaker turns elsewhere. The final four lines take us straight out to the road, the village store where a "truck loaded with hay" has stopped, its bales stacked and ordered, the work done and the world put right. "I wish you would look at the hay—" Kenyon writes in the lowest key possible, "the beautiful, sane and solid bales of hay."

I have an advantage, living in the Midwest in a medium-sized town where driving through farmland to get anywhere is always required. So I know what one sees through the windshield in that "magic hour" of the filmmaker or any other time of day in fall: timothy, alfalfa, red clover bound up large and compact, lying in the fields for later, winter into spring, for the livestock. Kenyon's choice of "sane" strikes me as perfectly keyed, the opposite of tone-deaf, an absolute *unflash* in its single-stress reserve and reach. Her linking it to "beautiful" is a new way to understand that beaten-to-death word, this sanity that literally bales up against hunger-to-come and quiets fear. Repetition adds depth and slows the urgency of "look at the hay," the central image taken up again in the last line's "sane and solid bales of hay," thus doing that Harvey Gross thing, the repeat making a "voiced pause" to lengthen the moment.

The singular pressure on every word of that wish, "I wish you would" is a most interior ache in the speaker against her outward plea—*look*, she insists—and the human sweep coming next. All suggest real time and real landscape. *Bales of hay*; to name that is to see that, and just hearing the phrase floats a kind of pictograph aftersound that never quite stops. (I, for one, can't drive by a field with such bales now without thinking *sanity*.) To say that hard image conveys this discovery best would be right, for Kenyon at least. Her careful build throughout the poem is how memory builds. She instructs our eye to the weight of things; a spare use of adjective and changed perspective shades and shows her own troubled mind until we're down to only a "wish" and those bales. Their beauty. Their solace. The fact is, it takes years to let one's images just *be* without editorial intrusion—*keep your mitts off!*—leaving them to their silence and pull, particularly at closure. Another equation then: confidence=humility=a trust generous enough to allow the world its way.

Jane Kenyon has company in this solitary passage filled with sepia light where image and even bits of story assume a fitful depth, enough to usher us out of the poem, directly into trance. There's George Oppen and Larry Levis. There's Jean Valentine. And Tom Andrews is a poet who barely survives his own poems, so many cut to the edge. Their aftersound—what he erases and can't quite say—is immense. Thus the damning and mysterious "Ars Poetica" from his second book, *The Hemophiliac's Motorcycle*, goes this way:

> The dead drag a grappling hook for the living.
> The hook is enormous. Suddenly it is tiny.
> Suddenly one's voice is a small body falling
> through silt and weeds, reaching wildly . . .

Many things here. First, the poem ends by not ending, trailing off in an ellipsis. But go back to its verbs—the *drag*, the *is* and *is*, and that *is* again, equally emphatic, set to lead naturally to that ellipsis, whose earliest use, an implied verbal omission if not our typographical dotted version, is credited to Old Norse speakers dropping the verb "to be" as a kind of shorthand, and thereby to keep it nevertheless, the raw fact of *being* itself that any five-year-old knows; *look at me, look at me*, calling out to her parents. And there's an intriguing use of the ellipsis in the old computer language Perl, too, as "true while *x* but not yet *y*," which gets at the ghostly suspension implied by its use. Our glowing mothership, though, the *Oxford English Dictionary*, gives its original meaning as "to leave," but yes, there's also a *falling* in there somewhere. Tom Andrews sends his poem out by way of the ellipsis, a dreaming off or a dreaming on, an assertion he makes as if too scared to continue, or simply speechless-with-knowing. His terminal ellipse is obsessive, triggering, buoying up a haunted aftersound. It's here and though we *are* leaving the poem—my God, look back!—*all this follows us*. And face it: we knew it all along.

Proof is, first line, the dead themselves in a workaday posture, returned and armed with "a grappling hook for the living," done up to full authority by way of the end stop, a complete and unequivocal sentence. Two fully intact sentences, also end stopped, make a second line. And a quick reversal. The hook *is*, but it grows "enormous." It *is*, but it shrinks to "tiny." And "one's voice"—*one's* voice, surely that's a stand-in for the most intimate first person, singular and plural—is "small," is "a small body falling" into bad dream, into "silt and weeds" and every mad gesture. We've passed through a life, haven't we? Something is cycling, and won't ever quit.

It may be that all poems, given Tom Andrews' title, are secret Mobius strips that eventually scroll from dark to darker. But this one—we're definitely back at the start with that closure, the dead dragging a hook for us. We're wild for it by the final line, caught in an endless looping—the dead, the living, no, the dead who re-up in this awful half-light, again and again and again.

Can we stand it, how haunted poems can be? Or need to be? To end, then, may involve, as in Halliday's case, a looking back, startled; or as in Kenyon's, a near-hypnotic sense of image that goes beyond wonder; or that hook—don't even think about that hook. Or it might get trickier, a *seeming* closure that keeps us mulling and coming up for air. There's a simple reason for such trickery. Here's Roger Kamein again, his say on the subject: "When a resolution is delayed . . . when the composer plays on our sense of expectation . . . drama or suspense is created." Or—in the case of Beethoven and Brigit Pegeen Kelly—a thing unbearable, now looming vast.

And no, it isn't off the mark to mention these two names in the same breath. It only takes a second breath to add Kamein's idea to connect them, one that fascinates as trapdoors fascinate, or the sudden press of truth when someone apologizes, after claiming to misspeak. I mean the so-called *deceptive cadence*. This must be as familiar as breathing to serious players of any instrument, and certainly to Beethoven, who used it on more than one occasion, famously in what was nicknamed the "Emperor," his fifth Piano Concerto, Opus 73. A "deceptive" cadence, then, because the piece appears to be coming to a close; you even want it to, the nice dinner party that fills us up and calms us down and after a time, yes, we're ready to go home now, thank you. Or it can seem like one end of a phone call that's not yours but which you overhear. Frost mentioned this, too, when he wrote of his beloved "sentence sounds," his "sound of sense" a reference not to the exact meaning of words, but instead to the rush of them through a closed door as a purely sonic, emotive *read*. So pretend you are a third party, listening from another room as someone speaks into an old-fashioned kitchen phone on the wall. The one side you hear fractures to bare monosyllables, a familiar *yes, uh-huh, sure, sure, okay then*—a genuine musical cadence, a descent, as the call winds down. Or not. Most surprisingly, definitely not. It isn't over; they're not finished. *Oh, no kidding!* the voice you *can* understand picks up again. So there's a way back after all, much more to do before resolution or closure, whatever you want to call the well-earned end of conversation, poem, concerto.

To hear distinctly how Beethoven's version of a "deceptive cadence" actually sounds, there's Glenn Gould playing with the Toronto Symphony Orchestra, and you can tune it in on YouTube anytime you can't sleep and see Gould hover, glide, and nearly levitate over the piano as he—no other way to say it—*impersonates* these sounds. Well into the second movement, the shift comes in late, and if you're alert, you might agree with my son's urgent e-mail calling attention to the music's effect: "Listen to how the phrase wants to resolve to the tonic, hit the ground. Instead, it remains aloft. And continues."

My son's wording suggests a full narrative: *wants to* until *instead*, then *remains aloft*. The sound sweeps on anyway, for several tries really, out of this almost-ending. So—no, the music isn't stopping at all but welling big, and sometimes very trickily down and dark via a sudden minor key change, wherever that leads on its wayward way out. About his concerto, Beethoven said this: zero, nothing at all. But I wonder simply and dumbly long after the fact how it came about, this idea of a second chance at closure. Was it always in the cards? Or revised *into*, to mime a discovery actually lived by this composer who was notorious for working and furious reworking, rarely blessed with the apparent "first thought, best thought" of a Mozart. Beethoven wasn't completely deaf—not yet—when he wrote this concerto in 1809, after the French had bombarded the daylights out of Vienna, which could not have helped his ears very much. But lying in a cellar for most of that time, in wait, must have resembled the lowest passage in any music, and it may have forced a second listening and considering, his hunkering down to hear a future beyond what's broken and *almost* to end. He did write some words about those days in the cellar: "What a destructive, barren existence all round me, nothing but drums, cannons, human misery of every kind." And later: "I worked then for weeks in succession, but it seemed to me more for death than immortality."

Brigit Pegeen Kelly's "Song"—maybe the most narrative effort of this profoundly lyric poet—gives its title to her second collection to begin that book focused on a more recent instance of human misery. What matters in this poem is too far-reaching and has too many dimensions to get right in one sitting. I can start a list for later: her use of Frost's "sentence sounds," the long and short of that telling; her metaphor that opens inward; the presence of prosaic and lyric elements so gracefully merged you hardly know this is, at heart, a kind of documentary, a report of real foul play no matter how surreal the story of a girl's pet goat stolen and bloodied and killed, hung from a tree limb. A decapitated goat, in fact, and no, only the head in that tree, the body elsewhere, at a distance where it "lay by the tracks." More—"they missed each other," the body calling to the head, the head to the body, and in that we get a tender, gruesome echo from the twelfth century, St. Catherine's heart in Rome since then, her head, resting miles away in Siena.

Inside such mythic dreaming, there is a fiction writer's harder impulse to this very large poem, a backstory involving how the girl cared for the goat, the "warm milk" she gave to it, the daily brushing, the girl's dream of his growing "bigger, and he did." Still, Brigit Kelly's lyric energy is heart-shattering, and fearless. At the killing, at the goat's "torn neck" on which flies are "already filling their soft bottles," this poet does not flinch. And the lyric flares of detail continue: wind, stones, a train's horn in faint earshot, eyes of the goat "like wild fruit"— too many riches to recount. Meanwhile—such meanwhile!— the narrative itself is paced as commonplace, deliberate, involving repetition enough to ground and then to hypnotize: "they hurried" and then "they hurried" and the girl "walked and walked," she "called and called" and "somebody found the head" and "somebody found the goat's body," and so on. The stripped-down repeated word choice and syntax mime a deep aching, the monotone in that; we're stained and simplified ourselves, just in the act of listening.

Which is how this poem starts in the first place: "Listen," says the poet with no underscoring of italics, no fanfare of exclamation. Some fifty lines later, we're alerted in a different way: it's "nothing but a joke" she tells us. And a lot of us, were this our poem—dream on, MacDuff!—might have stopped right there, or after a bit of embellishment to show the boys as callous and despicable, keeping her bit about how they whistle and the iconic, allusion-loaded washing of their "large" hands for sure, a moral tale neatly clicking shut. That is, if only narrative demands guided the shape of this piece, given—as Russell Edson pointed out in an extraordinary essay that keeps coming back to me—how prose, as opposed to poetry, is finite, since it "flows *through* time," and given that things "disappear . . . into the end of the plot," prose so plainly "tragic": you can't go back, you know too much. The end now, *end of story* in the parlance of our day. But it's ancient too, the singing in this poem weighted from the start, the word *tragedy* coming out of Greek, a combination of *tragos* for "goat" and *ode* for "song"—the goat, after all, a common choice for ritual sacrifice—expressing the darkest vision imaginable, finally understood.

Or never to be understood. Because there's a crucial unknowing at work here—isn't that the basic lyric instinct? It's that time moves *around* poetry, Edson reminds us too, its sense is "of the permanent, of time held." Thus perhaps Tom Andrews's dead can't let go of their grappling hooks, *can't*, over and over, while Kenyon's bales of hay will never stop comforting. And so it might be that Beethoven rethinks, no, *unthinks* his first closure back to an almost-closure in his fifth concerto. His genius, then, is part refusal, part giving up, but in either case succeeds in opening a lyric space to find one more thing, just as Brigit Kelly's does in this poem. "Listen," she insists again, and "here is the point . . . / . . . It was harder work than they / imagined, this silly sacrifice." She gathers up the urgent visible details that follow as straightforward narrative to finish off the *story* but like Beethoven's *almost* ending, this too is deceptive. She isn't done with the *understory*, and moves into an aftersound impossibly inside the poem now as if we were the ones sleepwalking, half out of, then again and again back into this dream. From straight-forward narrative cut rhetorical and surreal, she brings up the otherworldly singing of the goat again, a sound that shadowed the poem earlier at least four times. (You can tell it's near the end, my cellist son tells me, when a theme from the start of a piece comes back.) "What they didn't know/" she writes, "Was that the goat's head would go on singing, just for them." Which does pick up the bad news stitched first into the two opening lines, where "a goat's head," she tells us, "hung there and sang."

Here's my point: how rare and astonishing to keep going past such temptations of closure, the sound of ending ready and will-ing. This poet tells us a huge additional thing these boys "didn't know" and would never guess. Therein lies the power, the sug-gestion of a future beyond the story *as is*, not pinned to its narra-tive grid of girl and goat and boys as *given*, most dark and public fact. All that is suddenly backdrop. The poem opens to a com-plexity, an understanding unthinkable earlier when our hearts went straight for the girl and her loss. How something can be both solace and punishment, ruthlessly particular and calmly heroic, is a mystery so wrong that it's right, a hopeless mix. And those boys, the future will find them—like the rest of us now—haunted to the core because "they would learn to listen," and to

> Wake in the night thinking they heard the wind in
> the trees
> Or a night bird, but their hearts beating harder.
> There
> Would be a whistle, a hum, a high murmur, and, at
> last, a song,
> The low sound a lost boy sings remembering his
> mother's call.
> Not a cruel song, no, no, not cruel at all. This song
> Is sweet. It is sweet. The heart dies of this sweetness.

As for poetry then—is *closure* even in its lexicon? Here, now: yet another very deceptive cadence is in the making. I mean, to think *past* ending, *about* ending, as if that could end anything. Sure, go at it. I dare you. Good luck.

But some poems we never get out of.

Seeing Things

I begin with three ancient premises I almost believe. One: the dead move among us. Two: there is the thinnest veil between the things we see and the secret, heart-stopping place those images open to, and only image, the beloved particular, allows entry. Three: that hidden place is the source of poetry, of any art really, and tapping that requires two conflicting states of mind at once—vigilance and a kind of half-sleep, thinking and not thinking at all. I realize this sounds archaic and even unhinged, and that's probably the best I can hope for. It may sound familiar, a cliché really to those who came of age in the quasi-mystic mood music mindset of the late 1960s, early 70s—or those who didn't, both. It may smack of the worst sort of religiosity whose impulses, given my lapsed pre– and post–Vatican II Catholichood, should make me recoil, or laugh out loud in sad amazement: the dead, right here, now? A veil between worlds? Better to move quickly to more immediate things: supper, or getting the tires rotated, or having that sweet chat with someone grateful or complaining about the everyday work of the day, whatever its exhausting detail.

Or I could counter-presume and zero into the smaller, more rational side of my *almost* believing such things, and say no, the dead are quite dead. Forget them. And say there is no veil. The only worry *is* the surface; that's the *beloved* in such particulars, those images so close, so vividly remembered. And I could say there is no half mind in this process, nothing conflicting at all about the trance that art requires. We go full throttle or we go nowhere. Wake up into it. Drink tea or coffee. Write poems directly off that most shiny point of attention.

But this is mere overture—the shorthand of the longhand that keeps bothering me about this mysterious process: to see things, to see *through* them in order to write anything that lasts. Every bit of this has to do with image, the beloved particular. And I miscounted: four premises now—the dead, the veil, the hidden place, the wily, half-alert way into trance. So I begin again—this essay actually a fugue, a flight—but now with story, suggestion, example—and hope, exactly the kind that farmers in Papua, New Guinea once had, planting stones, round ones, as wide as the hand that held them so the tiniest seeds, not sure of how large they could grow, would take notice.

It's closing in on winter as I write this; I can see out the upstairs window the massive tulip tree two houses over where it towers over a neighbor's roof. It's dropped leaves, no longer what it was all summer in a lush green shimmer. The sky is streaking blue and white behind it this morning, still November. We might easily say *stark*, the great rising trunk. And delicate—*arterial*, down to a network, veins and even capillaries tangled, those branches going every which way. We might say it's merely—vastly—a simple x-ray of what it was, which would mean as I stare at it, at this thing once behind, hidden in what it used to be, I'm still *solving for X* somehow, some unlikely *into* this process, and *through*.

So I'm starting in backward on my list of premises, the unsettling way into trance. Which is where I imagine Wilhelm Röntgen almost stood, the German physicist who in 1896 discovered the X-ray, a faint, greenish beam—not light in any sense he knew—inexplicably passing through paper, cloth, wood, even human flesh—his own hand, then his wife's—to press itself fluorescent against the wall. But certain densities stopped it. Metal, for one. His wife's wedding ring hovers in the famous photograph of this moment. Bones in those fingers, the ghostly traces *inside* where the ray couldn't pass, where its absence in the photograph is simply blacked out, immediately a premonition to those gothic-minded Victorians. In fact, Bertha Röntgen is said to have "shuddered," horrified at seeing "her own skeleton." And Röntgen himself, who won the first Nobel prize in 1901 for his trouble, and after whom the world wanted to name this mysterious light, kept stubborn, insisting on his original impulse, that this force, this whatever-it-was be forever called the *X-ray* to honor that continuing sense of *solving for*. Enshrined in the name then: that moment of curiosity before the actual thing, that lab in late November when he stood by himself unnerved and astonished, the first on the planet to see such luminance.

Underscore that. And the Röntgens' solitude too, a most unlit ordinary room, windows sealed off for the work at hand. Darken that amazement further, take willfulness out of it, and we might get to Emerson, his realization once "crossing the bare common" alone in winter "at twilight" that he was inexplicably "glad to the brink of fear." Or so he wrote in an essay that triggered in a very young T. S. Eliot a similar shock though not glad at all, and far stranger: a noisy Boston street for that poet—if we believe his biographer, Lyndall Gordon—one usual day in 1910 abruptly *x-rayed* to an entirely different state. His poem "Silence," written when he was twenty-two and not published in his lifetime, seems beyond an account of an extraordinary afternoon walk, more the dangerous beginning of a whole poetic:

> Along the city streets
> It is still high tide
> Yet the garrulous ways of life
> Shrink and divide
> With a thousand incidents
> Bred and debated:—
> This is the hour for which we have waited—
>
> This is the ultimate hour
> When life is justified.
> The seas of experience
> That were so broad and deep,

So immediate and steep,
Are suddenly still.
You may say what you will,
At such peace I am terrified.
There is nothing else beside.

The eye plays tricks, of course; perhaps Eliot's vision—the terror of that moment's stillness, how those streets "shrink and dissolve"—has nothing whatever to do with poetry. The eye substitutes. It imagines. In sight's delicate mechanics, absence and presence, things seen then dissolving, changed somehow in the second look, the second thought—all this has a very physical counterpart in how the eye actually works. Cheap proof for this is the visual test in every Psych 101 textbook, the famous *is-it-a-vase?* or merely two human profiles face to face, depending how long one stares or how one arranges, then rearranges expectations, i.e., *gives up* expectations. So we keep learning it's all about the eye taking up clues, being reasonable with them, then going looser somehow. Any chair, for instance—if one were to draw that—would mean horizontal lines for the seat, a vertical stress with the pencil up and down for the legs, for the definite edges of the back.

But absence itself is a presence. Artists call this "negative space," which is to say, what's *not* there has a shape, is, in fact, the very thing that makes any sort of positive space credible at all, the so-called "nameable" objects that seem to leap out and make up any drawing. But look farther, past the obvious hard lines into those parts of the chair one can't see—the world of air under the seat, the back built so it forces a curve, empty, for the shoulders. Draw that. This is often an assignment in studio classes, the chair one is careful *not* to see, its legs and back and seat come onto the page regardless, simply by way of the empty places now given boundary and edge. What's there, in short, is made visible, forced into being by what is entirely *not*. One could lose what little sense one might have thinking this way, I suppose, like staring too long at an Escher print, or trying to figure for good where the first and last edge of a Mobius strip might be. Back and forth, there/not-there, "the seas of experience . . . suddenly still." Eliot's glimpse goes even beyond that choice and freezes us. Like him, we are stopped short, falling through, solving for X, into more hidden mysteries.

An immense part of this poetic, if we can call it that, is the *unbidden*, this quality of *gift*, however dark, the it-came-to-me-I-had-nothing-to-do-with-it jolt of realization. Even Röntgen, his lab carefully readied, making an occasion for *something* to happen, was nevertheless completely surprised by his discovery. One might frame that as trademark romantic, where the unseen, a belief in that, is often the default position. Surely John Keats meant something close to this when he held up "negative capability" as one of the crucial things poets must aid and abet in themselves, the ability to remain "in uncertainties, mysteries, doubts; without any irritable reaching after facts and reasons." The ability to see, and wait until caught genuinely unaware.

Anthony Hecht's much anthologized piece "The Hill" is such a shining, serious example of this visionary moment, I hesitate even to bring it up. The poem is characteristically urbane, well-spoken and traveled. It's set in Italy "where this sort of thing can occur," the speaker mentions at once. What sort of thing? So we are whetted and launched on a high promise, into a self-deprecation, this vision "nothing like Dante's" he insists he saw. To get to that point, we are led backward to the busy, beautifully made groundwork, what calls up this "warm sunlit piazza" in the first place, before the vision: friends and the "fretwork of shadows," the "bargaining" in the street over everything, it seems, "books, coins, old maps, cheap landscapes." So it goes. The sound and sights of a life, of many lives, common, unspectacular, even given the great Farnese Palace seen, barely, at the corner of the eye. And then we're abruptly back to Eliot's moment, past Emerson's, because "it happened, the noises suddenly stopped. / And it got darker." And we understand that the vast cacophony of the Roman street is over, the Palace vanished, and "in its place

> Was a hill, mole-colored and bare. It was very cold,
> Close to freezing, with a promise of snow.
> The trees were like old ironwork gathered for scrap
> Outside a factory wall. There was no wind,

And the only sound for a while was the little click
Of ice as it broke in the mud under my feet.
I saw a piece of ribbon snagged on a hedge,
But no other sign of life. And then I heard
What seemed a crack of a rifle. A hunter, I guessed;
At least I was not alone. But just after that
Came the soft and papery crash
Of a great branch somewhere unseen falling to
    earth.

A stanza break allows us to collect these bare-bone particulars, lengthening the pause just enough. "And that was all," we're told, "except for the cold and silence / that promised to last forever, like the hill." Exactly the place, in short, where Eliot stopped, too overwhelmed to go past such summary.

Only Hecht doesn't stop. The world returns—the sound of bartering, the look of "sunlight and friends." Just a week of being "scared by what I'd seen." Then ten years pass, in the poem and apparently in the life. But recovery isn't what it seems. "I remembered that hill," the poet tells us in language whose spare beauty (so richly quiet, this iambic pentameter line) matches the seeming out-of-the-blue hard clarity of its meaning. "It lies just to the left / Off the road north of Poughkeepsie, and as a boy / I stood before it for hours in the wintertime."

So a third level swamps, floods this piece. This gift of seeing, of seeing *through*, and seeing *through yet again*, from the busy marketplace to a scene stripped, isolated, full of dread, and then past Emerson's glad fear, certainly past the young Eliot's premonition of the wasteland waiting for him to enter and live to tell of, to this inward *return*, a childhood place, a lived moment. An X-ray of an X-ray. *Make the familiar strange* is one of the great dictums of art, past Ezra Pound's plea for the new. But stranger still to come back and see what is too close for elegant commentary in what stuns, even terrifies.

A few years ago I was lucky, happening upon a very odd article about a guy—presumably the author, Jeffery Keel—his account of working outside all summer, maintaining filtration pipes somewhere in Wisconsin. But the piece was really about a cat.

And if one X-rayed that, it was in fact about hunger, Keel's careful observations of that animal, a former house cat—"My only companion," he writes straight out, "recently abandoned to the fields." What fascinates is Keel's fresh eye as he watches the cat quickly adapt, beginning to stare and stalk on his own, fueled by this new thing, hunger. Struck by this transformation, Keel himself begins to fast, a kind of solidarity with the animal, and he gradually grows astonished. Sounds and scents, "the drone of a tractor" far off, the "smell of earth, wildflowers, and moist decay," all seem wildly amplified as he grows hungrier. "It was as if Nature had turned up the volume," he writes, "exaggerated its movements and illuminated the colors of the landscape." The climax comes a week into the fast as Keel, following the cat's stare out over the pasture—not at all the first time he's tried it, always before noticing only "a tangle of vegetation." But now he *sees* it, how that "tuft of grass quivered against the undulating movement of the grass." A mouse! We discover that via the wise and agile cat as he runs and pounces and brings back his prey. "From that moment on," Keel writes, "the fields, which had once appeared tranquil, came alive." Until, that is, he's back to solid food again, and everything returns—"subsided" is the word he uses with genuine regret—"to within the usual realm of my senses." *Subsided* then, the veil in place again between these worlds, human and nonhuman, the known and what is commonly unknowable, out of reach, not even an option.

Of course hunger and visions have a long very unsecret history together in virtually any culture—the Arab stories of struggles that any poorly fed desert traveler might have with *jinn*, an evil spirit, or St. Teresa's moments of hallucinatory prayer especially during Lent, or the Tibetan ritual of *chod*, where a young fasting would-be shaman goes to a desolate spot to await instruction. Hours of stress in whatever bodily form loom large in this context, the Inuit's *kayakangst*, for instance, described by anthropologist Weston LaBarre as "coming to the hunter out alone in his kayak in a featureless sea," a "trancelike lowering of consciousness" with an "hypnotic fixing." Other near-pathological conditions, however temporary, ignited by drugs of whatever legal or illegal stripe, are known for bringing on imaginary wonders, some angelic, many decidedly not.

But this story of a pasture in Wisconsin is not really a vision in that sense, unless we include the Arctic kayaker's "hypnotic fixing" in some way. The cat—and eventually the human teller of the tale—see exactly what *is*, what's there, howbeit weirdly enlarged and narrowed at the same time. What this small fable does—and it has that *fable* feel: man and cat, hunger and the hunt, world fleshed out in abrupt, super real detail—is move us vividly into something close to what I want to call *poetic time*. And not dream really, closer to daydream, the poet, I suppose, pretty much the "dreamer in broad daylight" characterized by Freud in the work he did on the experience of writers, though certainly what I mean lies under the usual wistful Walter Mitty projections of love and success anyone might bring to this. For the record, the state itself is called an "hypnagogic experience" by psychologists, one of whom, Herbert Silberer, described the daydream's two parts: "drowsiness and the effort to think, the first a passive state, not subject to the will," which is to say, one finds oneself in that slight off but quite real netherworld between utter wakefulness and sleep—or between hunger and something past hunger that opens in very physical ways by means of images that remain and haunt—the drone of the tractor in the story, say, or the scent of "moist decay." The mind, then, is a kind of hovercraft. One begins to *see* differently, an intensification. And it's a matter of the beloved particular again, what poems are made of.

An obvious example here might be Sylvia Plath's well-known poem "Tulips," itself about illness, *seeing through* that curious state, by definition unsettled and between worlds, the happy clockwork of well-being shot to hell. The speaker in the poem is reduced to a hospital room, the details of her stripped-down fate—the family in a photograph "their little smiling hooks," and the "bright needles" that bring "numbness" to her. "Stupid pupil," she tells us of her eye in this lockdown which nevertheless "takes everything in." And it does, but so oddly that we feel a large shock with each small adjustment of the lens. And it isn't a lockdown, of course, but a place constantly released, refigured by a key element in Plath's genius—metaphor—the speaker "a thirty-year cargo boat," or "a pebble" the nurses tend as water might. Or she is a nun, and "never so pure."

But it's the tulips—the not-so-beloved particulars here—that rise up and overwhelm and transform this troubling daydream, this very "controlled hallucination" as Robert Lowell, Plath's teacher, once defined any poem worth the name. These tulips are "too red"; they "breathe" through their paper "like an awful baby." They "talk to my wound"; they are finally "a dozen red lead sinkers around my neck," or worse somehow, "dangerous animals . . . opening like the mouth of some great African cat." In short, "it corresponds," Plath says, but "they are subtle." The poet's attention here is on target, frightening and exact. Yet that sideways, wayward motion of half-sleep is here too. *That* fuels metaphor, this leap to some wild but, yes, *corresponding* elsewhere, envisioned so clearly in images that surprise us out of this room, out of this specific seemingly hopeless life, a loosening, a flight. But isn't it perfectly ordinary? These tulips in a sick room in their cheerful gift paper? Plath X-rays these flowers into something so strange we are *nowhere else but here* in this room, this poem, a genuine near-accident of thinking with its negative and positive, fully original charge.

And to get there? To arrive at that near-accident? I can't help reading Laura Jensen's poem "I Want Some" in this light, a kind of *ars poetica*, the poem a place really, where we are equally distanced, but narrowed to

> . . . the porch of the abandoned house
> where a glassless window
> is propped open to ventilate.
>
> And though the air floats around
> where no one can poke a head out an
> upstairs window and shake down a mop
> and say, no!
>
> I will not steal some.
>
> I have stood
> so many times just down the street
> and peered
> to where a bus should return
> like a stone you dropped from a bridge
> coming back to you, that I feel I know

this poor lost house—
that developed tilt, that air
of studied mystery, that appeal.

But I will not steal some
before I stand and wait.

I want some.
Oh, how I do.

The desire here is meticulous and large, both willful and—
unlike Plath's poem—consciously kept back, everything precari-
ous in that emphatic moment of *almost* knowing. The speaker
would enter a house, but will not; does *want* some, but won't ask.
"I have stood / so many times . . . / and peered / to where a bus
should return." she tells us, the experience of watching *for*, of
trying to *see through*, such hours behind her that now give reason
and purpose to any imagining. Thus, "I feel I know / this poor
lost house— / that developed tilt, that air / of studied mystery,
that appeal."

But. This small word coming next is the great creaking hinge
of the hidden trap door in so many poems. You could, in fact,
triple that here—*but but but*—or cast it in italics or boldface,
though Jensen does not. Her tact is too great, her restraint too
immediate. "But I will not steal some/," she insists, "before I
stand and wait." Then the closure's flood, both quickened and
rooted by the hammered grace of the single-stressed words and
the shortest of lines, not to mention the public elegance of the
couplet shape, however ghostly and interior the utterance: "I
want some. / Oh, how I do." It's a stance that mines how difficult
it is to lift the veil, to ready oneself to pass through to that other
world—not really the self anymore, not anything predictable—
and find the poem that waits there.

This sense of deep process, the poem and its own how-to kit
somehow embedded inside it: I suddenly realize this is a vital
impulse in any poem I love, any poem I am witness to, hearing
a mind *thinking*, Elizabeth Bishop's profound wish for poems,
that they be a "mind-in-motion" taking image, idea apart, some-
thing beyond that, taking shape. John Berger said straight out:

art is a record of creation, not representation. And so it's the seeing, not so much the thing seen, that colors what is found for the page. This might be a given among neuropsychologists, of course, one of whom, Richard Gregory, stating simply that "objects are public and experience is private," a fact made clear to any of us visiting our hometown years after leaving and coming upon familiar sites—old house, old library, old bandshell in the park—altered but eerily the same. Either way, we're suddenly ghosts, our own small dramatic history there, pure smoke.

Still, this *looking again*, the double-take that makes memory, is something that fuels many cherished poems. Finding that hard stare, doing that, requires the patience that shines in Jensen's poem. This patience is rare but enters right into the process of making such things. I recall Ellen Voigt in an after-reading discussion once, thrown that classic bewildering question: how do you write poems? How do you keep one going through all the moves it has to make? In response, she went deep into specifics, taking up from her third book, *The Lotus Flowers*, the poem "Nightshade," that apparently seamless creature. But she was X-raying it back, telling us with considerable dismay how the piece had stopped her cold for quite some time. Because? First half, she told us, full story: a beloved dog, accidentally poisoned by its owner's mistaken dosage, though the intent—a bit of strychnine as a "tonic" to sharpen its hunting instincts—was commonplace. Thus the "sobbing children" so carefully presented in the piece. It was "their father" who had done the deed, after all, their dog, their front porch under which the stricken animal had crawled to die. The problem? The worry some poets have about all narrative, I suppose, be the story tragic or not: its automatic impulse to contain. Because it *was* all used up, Ellen Voigt implied. The tale told, end of story! Where else to take it?

So she let it sit; basically she gave up. And only much later, there came the brilliant readjustment of the lens. She *knew* how to go further, how to break that surface fact. And the seam is disguised mid-stanza, the thread picked up by a simple but profound shift in point of view. No longer is it cool omniscience, but an abrupt *I*, first person, the claim thrilling and decisive, kept barely in place by urgent dashes, the speaker stepping forth, owning up:

And I loved my father—

I was among the children looking on—
and for years would not forgive him . . .

Two jolts then: of person, third to definite first, a fierce launch that allows the poem's second great orbit, from story toward idea, toward sweep, which profoundly disrupts the very shape of things. "Without pure evil in the world," she can tell us now, "there was no east or west, no polestar / and no ratifying dove." The speaker returns then to memory, to other specifics of the past soaked now in this new troubling vision. She sees the girl she was, playing piano "in the small white house for hours," caught forever after between two endless, warring points of reference, two songs, "one in a major, the other in a sad, minor key." And so Hecht's brooding mole-colored hill comes back, sharing the multiplicity of any given instant when so clearly *seen*, a single moment that can vastly enlarge and alter time.

One of my Purdue colleagues, two buildings over from mine in the German Department, works on image. (I love that phrase, that scholars "work on" people, on ideas. *Oh, I never work on Trollope anymore*, I heard someone say before a recent faculty meeting, and I pictured her smartly stripping off her surgical gloves.) But Beate Allert does work on image, and she told me this: images are unfinished thoughts. I gather that's a good thing, "unfinished" in this sense not the clueless child who will someday, with luck, become the witty, all-knowing (or at least half-knowing) adult but the child who really *is* father to the man, wise beyond—or rather *before*—wisdom. What I value in her remark is how images come first, that treasures are buried in them. Whether these riches are extracted, and how—here poets and scholars surely part ways.

To return to Richard Gregory, there's this morsel from his classic work *Eye and Brain*, which sets the primacy of visual image so far back in time, we almost lose it. "The regions of the cerebral cortex concerned with thought," Gregory writes, are comparatively juvenile. They are self-opinioned by comparison with the ancient regions of the brain giving survival by seeing. The perception system does not always agree with the rational thinking cortex. For the cortex educated by physics, the moon's distance is 390,000 km.; to the visual brain it is a few hundred metres. Though here the intellectual cortical view is the correct one, the visual brain is never informed, and we continue to see the moon as if it lies within our grasp. The visual brain has its own logic and preferences, which are not yet understood by us cortically. Some objects look beautiful, others ugly; we have no idea for all the theories which have been put forward why this should be so. The answer lies a long way back in the history of the visual part of the brain, and is lost to the new mechanisms which give us our intellectual view of the world.

So a question: with all the dangers—the just-plain-wrong so-called "moon effect" among them—why are we so often drawn to image to spark and guide the poems and stories we write or read? Gregory insists elsewhere that "visual perception is seldom ambiguous." We can trust it, he says. Really? Yes—and no. (I have heard Donald Hall say that image is the most easily translated, unlike ideas trussed up in their abstraction.) And yet how do we understand those hardcore particulars that sometimes go ambiguous, beyond that vase and/or two human profiles business, to enrich the image, the *lethal* beauty of that greenish beam in the darkened lab in 1896, or those smiles in Plath's photograph, "little smiling hooks" after all. Or how Eliot's dizzy, workaday street is actually a disguise, a shroud over the void that waits in all of us. "Ambiguous figures give us no clue of which bet to make," Gregory goes on, "so it never settles one bet." And this is a "curious disadvantage," he says, at times even "disastrous." I'm not so sure. It may be the beginning of art, that trap door opening just when we were thinking everything figured out, the story fixed, the view frozen. So the mind seeks some other way to understand and break up the tidy surface, to deepen complexity: a father loved but no, I'm sorry, never forgiven, major and minor chords in endless coexistence and dissonant, troubling, true.

Poets see—and see past things. And the dead often become part of this, whether one wills it or not. Think of Li-Young Lee, finding his father again and again, this ghost who enters so much of his work, the early poem "Eating Alone" one example, where first it's simply a bare garden, the end of the day, a cardinal, a cellar door, "the icy metal spigot" from which the speaker drinks. Then, in that gesture, the shift to memory, a walk "beside my father / among the windfall pears." And that pear? Here is the great turn, a close-up strange, surreal but clearly "a rotten pear" now remembered in his father's hand, and a hornet "spun crazily, glazed in slow, glistening juice." A full two lines keeps us there and, of course, the hornet is slow, drunk, darkly jubilant. We're deep into trance because of it, this thing seen in such an interior way that we're ready: the dead do come back. "It was my father I saw this morning," Lee writes,

> waving to me from the trees. I almost
> called to him, until I came close enough
> to see the shovel, leaning where I had
> left it, in the flickering, deep green shade.

The shovel, real and forgotten, transformed here *back* to itself, is logical, is Gregory's more recent part of the brain at work to return the daily rhythms: supper now in the poem, rice steaming. But it's Lee's willingness to step into trance—via the that glazed hornet, the too sweet rotting pear—so death can enter to enliven, to make our small reach ancient, moving forward and back, however briefly.

In Frost's singular poem "After Apple Picking," such a moment changes everything; intent, process, where any of us— writer or reader—might end up. "I cannot rub the strangeness from my sight," Frost tells us,

> I got from looking through a pane of glass
> I skimmed this morning from the drinking trough
> And held up before the world of hoary grass.
> It melted, and I let it fall and break.
>
> But I was well
> Upon my way to sleep before it fell,
> And I could tell
> What form my dreaming was about to take.

But he could not. The rest of the poem proves that. Just a glimpse again. And nothing any of us—including Frost, I suspect—might plan or predict.

So the trance, the veil, the hidden place. And the dead—who can be stubborn, who can return. There are things, of course, one can never explain.

Once, in my mid-twenties—I was in grad school, biking home in winter—Massachusetts, so it was cold, snowy; it was almost dusk. I felt eager to get there, down the driveway at last, our apartment up the stairs in the back, past the bright bedroom window of Allison Cook, our eighty-two-year-old neighbor for whom my husband and I took turns preparing dinner every night, one of our part-time jobs. Hers was the front apartment, the spacious rooms of the lower floor in what once was a stately house: two fireplaces, an expansive front porch, leaded windows, the serious and original kitchen.

As I biked up the drive, Mrs. Cook, as usual, was reading in bed, her light on her book. But there beside her on the divan before the fireplace was a curious figure—young, curly-haired, lithe, beautiful really. Male or female, it was hard to tell though in the split second I passed on my beat-up Schwinn, I thought *male*, and he was looking down, chin in his hands, apparently deep in thought, *deciding something*, I suddenly decided. But the whole scene, it wasn't quite right—not Mrs. Cook, most gracious of hosts, ignoring her guest, not this figure, poised so intently, so quietly, not looking at her now. All this in a flash as I biked by, the mind trying to *read* and coming up with nothing that worked, my *why* and *why* and *why* until in a dark half-second I knew, I swear it then and now, it was Death I was seeing, and wrong, *wrong* to see that, I had no right—but *Death*—it was clear now. And he was deciding whether to take her. I turned the corner then, breathless, certain, stricken.

I walked up the stairs. In an hour, it would be my turn to make her supper. It took all my courage to walk down there and through the unlocked back hallway which connected our parts of the house. I opened the door. I could hear the news. Mrs. Cook had the TV on, which was simply what she did that time of day. I entered the kitchen and there was her *Joy of Cooking* propped open on the marble-topped counter. She wanted chipped beef on toast, a favorite. I fell into our routine, making her drink: two shots of whiskey, a teaspoon of orange marmalade, ice, a little water, and walked it to the living room. We chatted—the news, the weather. Soon it would snow again. I couldn't help asking: your afternoon—how was it?

Nothing much going on, she said, mainly I just read more of the Conrad.

You feeling okay?

Not bad, she half-shrugged. But you know, about an hour or so ago, it was awful, I felt pretty much done-in. But, well—her old cheer coming back—I'm fine now.

It was days before I began to think I wasn't crazy, at least not in that way. And weeks before I told my husband about it. You won't believe what I saw, I began the way all such confessions probably begin. We were at an art exhibit, sitting on one of those long wooden benches. And what he said still charms me: how nice that Death will come for Mrs. Cook as a beautiful young man. Really, she'll be so happy to go off with him.

For my part, I still feel what I witnessed completely unearned. I'm not in the habit of such things. Somehow, I had intruded and saw something I wasn't meant to see. I wanted just to get home and settle in for the night, any thoughts in my head the vapid urgencies of my day. But the veil lifted, world within world, no chance to understand any of it in the usual way. And the greater wonder—how quickly everything came back: my breathing normal, the bread toasting for Allison Cook's creamed chipped beef, the news blaring in the next room, and later, my husband's quirky, matter-of-fact pleasure in the story.

But I repeat: I saw something I was never meant to see.

A final premise, then, about writing, about poetry in particular: one must go further, beyond safety where nothing quite resolves. Go past where it still burns or chills, beyond the point one imagines one has something to say.

Is and Was

Once is a word most suspect. Once that could have been a sentence I was sent to the blackboard to diagram.

So the chalk in my hand makes a line, here to here, a horizon. On it, I write *once*, first position, then the crossbar coming down before the quiet, most sure of itself verb-to-be, that modest *is*, a linking verb, emphatic linchpin followed not by a line straight up to keep it apart but one that slashes left, leans back, a secret trap door. Then *word* coming third, pinned down by such sudden attention, its modifiers below on their slanted lines, the most indefinite *a*, the most suspect of adjectives, that *suspect* there. *Once is a word most suspect.*

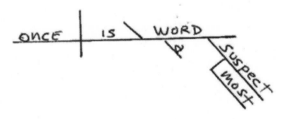

I'm a kid. I step away from the board to read to my classmates, no idea at all—any of us—what I'm saying. The verb *is*—any grammar book will tell you—simply renames the subject. *Once* is called *word* and here, in diminishing returns, is one of many, *a* word not *the* word which—most daringly of all—is suspect. *Equals* suspect. Equals *never to be vouched for, not really.* Equals *I made it up.* Or *do I remember?* Or *someone remembers.* It could be all three.

You know those stories? goes the story of the famous writer before his class. Those stories, he is saying, you know, where a man looks out a window longingly, dreamily back to the boy he

36

was? Back to a key he could feel in his pocket. To a dog racing ahead long ago in the woods. And he—that man—hovers there. So the key is radiant, isn't it? And the dog is still wet from the river. You know those stories? the teacher is asking his students again. I hate those stories.

And poetry, I think. Of all the reasons to hate that too, is this one of them? Spin back then, in some quickened expanse of *all poems*, bits there flaring up and buzzing. And of course, poems *recollect in tranquility*, don't they? *Emotion* in that tranquility, to be exact. Thank you, Wordsworth, who put that in the job description. So we poets too keep dreaming there. (Hate that, hate that! says the famous writer.)

Oh yes, we're busted all right. Busted, busted. . . .

Memory then. But of course such a thing exists, and *is* the linchpin of poetry. Everything we are is beholden to it. It's built right into language, past tense and all the deliberate ways to score that, to break that open and split hairs—past perfect and present perfect, the pluperfect and so on. The older we get, the more memory clouds or clears what we see. We don't merely imagine its pressure, don't always let it slide into an overwhelming terrible weight or pure squish, though both are dangers. *How* it works in poems: the *how* is crucial. Because memory's ache is enormous. And greedy.

Technically, in visual art at least, there were centuries when just looking at things accurately in terms of time and space—this part close, that part farther away—seemed about impossible. A 3-D world reduced to a flat surface? Only two ways for an artist to try for that really. We've seen those medieval paintings, the dark or luminous everything-happening-at-once kind, those frozen figures, saints or angels or mere mortals however exalted among us in stylized dress with gold leaf and busy textures shrunken down to show what is closer, or overlapping to show that, the larger figures blocked by those smaller, just slightly in front. But everyone's stolidly floating there, pretty much the same eternal moment on wood panel or plaster or stone, no precise way to understand what comes, what's immediate vs. what waits out there. Distant line of land or sea—what kind of thing is that?— though there it must have been *this whole time*, in real daylight at the edge of a field or beyond the city wall. How to nail it, in two dimensions? Which is to say, imagine this gradual historical shift. No, it's abrupt, we're told: the end of a dramatic, near claustrophobic way of looking at anything, this last medieval moment before *perspective* took hold as a *discovered* thing, then a willed thing, unto habit. An Italian architect, sculptor, genius troublemaker is setting up his easel backward in the Duomo's center doorway in Florence, about 1425. He's placing a mirror there too, a smallish sort of mirror, inches, maybe 12 by 12, tops, because they're expensive. Quirky, the whole business. Just an experiment, he might have said to anyone passing by.

I love the mirror thing. In the crude illustrations of this moment, it's Filippo Brunelleschi doing this, largely inventing our modern idea of perspective, thus changing the way a thing is seen, or at least the way artists *get it down* to mark depth— foreground, background, the long stretch to whatever far-off river. In those illustrations, there's always one very wide easel. It faces the Baptistery behind him as he stands in the doorway of the Duomo, the cathedral with its massive dome he himself as chief architect built, though still at that time under construction, its angles-to-be and curves he must have already known by heart. On the easel to his right was a blank panel of wood, and directly before him, that mirror in which the Baptistery loomed up. And Brunelleschi—careful—painting now its exact lines onto the panel to his right though it must have been tricky, his head squarely in the center of that mirror, totally *in the way*, his leaning to one side or the other, maybe angling the thing a little to edge himself out, to pretend he wasn't there at all.

Finally, the painting finished: here's the clincher. He bores a small hole—*the size of a lentil*, it's said, opening *to a ducat*— on the blank side of his painting as friends, fellow artists, god knows who else stood waiting in the street; they must have been. Because every version of this story mentions the curious many, one by one, turned to face the Baptistery, then told to hold the panel up close, brushwork side *out*, to look through that hole from behind, Brunelleschi setting up the mirror in the viewer's other hand to reflect the painting, reversing left and right to a proper correspondence. See the Baptistery in the mirror? The one I just painted? Brunelleschi must have said over and over with such flourish. Now this! And like a carnival magician, thrilled by cheap spectacle, he whisked away the mirror to reveal the real-life thing, the Baptistery itself, identical to anyone staring through the peephole: foreground, background, the way it actually *looked* on the panel in that mirror. Amazing!—to them, if not to us. And though the Greeks and Romans had their way with it, here was *perspective*, refound after the darkest of ages, fresh as insight, the depth and complication of things, back and back, all the right proportions flat out on the surface, allowing the illusion: it is, it fully is *just like that*.

Of course, the whole business gets vastly complex. Of course Brunelleschi, in doing this, broke the mystery down to brilliant mathematics, a sharp-toothed vanishing point, all the ways it *means* and keeps meaning to draw something and *get it right*, the proper sequence, what's here—*this*—against what's left behind or in the future. And rules to follow. Things to measure and compute. And measure again. It became the rage to see clearly like that, a key to the Renaissance and its new state of mind. Next to an earlier medieval image of cities—ghostly towers and walls huddled together, overlapping, seemingly airless—there is, for example, the "Map with a Chain," a painting of the period pointed out by art historian Samuel Edgerton: Florence at a distance, a few years after Brunelleschi's experiment. In it, one sees a city suddenly understood from a higher, cleaner vista, its mountains anon, its bridges and river sweep, its neighborhood upon neighborhood so coolly managed, the sky above released to a deliberate endlessness now.

But this haunts me: Brunelleschi in that primal moment, his back to the Baptistery, his head, his reflection in that mirror so annoying, continually *in the way* as he painted, his eye catching his own eye too often. *Perspective* then—here's another definition: the massive will power it must have taken to see anything in spite of that head, to keep the huge self out of it.

When Eavan Boland began to work German poetry into English, pieces written about lives shattered by the Second World War, the fact is—quite literally—a very small self triggered it. In the introduction to her book of those translations, she recalls the child she was, listening to the two young women her parents had hired for a few years after the war, still teenagers really, fled from the stricken German countryside, sisters so busy—*beschaftigt*—in that Dublin kitchen with its peat fire, its damp laundry, its soup and bread. Memory's press and release, those shards of a language nearly unknowable but adrift in the air: "intaglios," she says of her impressions, "cut . . . in my consciousness." The door they opened for the poet that Boland was to become "led from our ordinary tea-time kitchen to the very heart of a broken Europe."

A remarkable thing, to make the leap that would allow those translations, but how matter-of-fact and astonishing, the child back there, repeating in wonder or just for something to do, the *eine zwei drei vier* when those sisters had a moment to offer her in the Irish dusk. A lens, then, a way in, a *conduit*, she says of language, language tied to poems she brings out of German in which we feel the weight of the smallest familiars—"a cup, a shoe, an open window, a village roof with missing slates." *Image*, George Oppen said in his "Statement of Poetics," "because image is the moment of conviction." And in that moment, that most transparent, wide-awake state, maybe the self *is* tiny. But on the force of the *other*, someone else remembering such things, an expanse wells up, is heady and distant even as it closes in, to include and sometimes take us beyond the poem. Boland tells it this way: "*that could have been me*, we suddenly think. *I could have been there.*" But I'll cut to the chase here: it is also—and largely so—the verbs, not *which* verbs exactly but their shifting *in time*, even unto their disappearing, wielding this mysterious power. Because "meaning is the instant of meaning," Oppen went on to say. That instant, that *click*, involves time. And verbs: a whole species of words we've invented to *mime* that click.

In one of her own poems, "The Parcel," Boland begins straightforward enough in present tense though almost immediately she looks back. "There are dying arts and / one of them is / the way my mother used to make up a parcel." Then a wealth of "how-to" detail: "Paper first," she says right off and into the next and next, the place of scissors in all this ballooning out as she takes her time to get us up to speed and into memory itself—

> Not a glittering let-up but a dour
> pair, black thumb-holes,

the shears themselves the colour of rained-
on steps a man with a grindstone climbed up
in the season of lilac and snapdragon
and stood arguing the rate for
sharpening the lawnmower and the garden pair
and this one. All-in.

New sentence: *All-in.* In its swift quirky fragmenthood, we hear that *spoken*, the moment wholly present in the sound. But the long winding previous sentence is itself a fragment, its verbs only secondary, quieted to modify the steps the man "climbed up," where he "stood arguing," the choice of syntax allowing that scene, that action to hover somewhere between past and present. Then with its full end stop after such meandering: *All-in.* The phrase flares up to bring us a moment of pure *being* though soon it's back to ordinary time—here, we're all adults here, just reading a poem, our job to join the speaker in witnessing the task and those details that follow in sequence.

Which is to say, it's story again; the twine *was braided*, the flame *held* to melt the sealing wax, the address she, the mother, *wrote*. And we follow obediently, watching as the mother gets on with the job at hand. But not for long because pretty quickly we're back to four rapid-fire nearly verbless fragments: "Names and places. Crayon and fountain pen. / The town underlined once. The country twice." Take that, Boland might as well say. Take that, childhood, memory itself a dying art, lost except in furious gestures. Then abruptly, with the most reasonable of complete sentences—"It's ready for the post, she would say"—we're back to more soothing remembrance though the present tense—*it's ready*—is loud even as it's lulled by the second verb to something slower—she *would say*—kept with affection. This curious *would* thing, from the old English *willen* meaning "wish, want, be willing," sweet habit in that, over and over—she would, she could, she always did that, didn't she?—grief barely present but it continues, built right into the verb tense to grow even larger as if, yes, the speaker too wishes and wants.

What Boland does next is breathtaking because it's utterly plain. A shift again to present tense—though aren't we still there in the past? It's what I've always called the *eternal present*, and here brilliantly cast into the imperative mood, direct address so we're collared into this and have no choice. It's that sad and that grave. And there's the public sensible sound of a complete sentence, a kind of *perspective* in that, Brunelleschi's cool artifice to effect real grace, verbs simple and objective in their command, the voice claiming itself plural now—*our* eyes—not really personal anymore, not threatened by nostalgia. It's an overvoice voice, a speaker who sees a long way and knows things, however stricken, and must say them. About such a parcel slipped into the post's burlap bag, an art—a world—"lost before we missed it"—

> See it disappear. Say
> this is how it died
> out: among doomed steamships and outdated trains,
> the tracks for them disappearing before our eyes,
> next to station names we no longer
> recognize. The sealing wax cracking.
> The twine unraveling. The destination illegible.

Such a dark epic move in what seemed a small and grateful lyric poem about the past. Things broken here grow bigger than anyone's life. Elegy: a mother, a childhood, an era. In the end only sentence shards remain, two of the three fragments clearly in the past but forever ongoing by way of their almost-verbs cast partial and ruined but still moving in their *i-n-g* form: this wax "cracking," the twine "unraveling," never to be stopped. All of it finally impossible to read.

In his poem "Route," George Oppen said it simply enough. "The context is thousands of days." And at the beginning of all this, when Aristotle took up the issue of time, he went right to that most credible entry, to *now*—our *now* in such a context, *the* now—the only point we all share and can be at least a little certain of. We can't help but stand here at the "boundary" he said, between something he called "the no-longer" and the "not-yet" though he claimed the moment so fleeting, so slippery, never quite real, never to earn the gravity of the great Past or Future. Still, why write poems at all if not from that peculiar place in the psyche where both sides flood to tangle and trouble, the future turning into past even as we stand and wonder? Boland's rained-on steps bring back the scissors man, eventually those doomed steamships and trains, the cracking, the unraveling *in progress.* Isn't this what it's like from here, in the present, this unsteady never-to-be-trusted region between the *no longer* and the *not yet?*

Our most daily sense of hour unto year and years is probably far less charged, even if we only half believe Oppen in his earlier poem "Route," that there's "nothing more real than boredom, its dreamlessness, the experience of time." And publicly, the ways we think of time—which is to say, our habits with it—are so orderly really. Consider the story, possibly the first handed down on the subject, a visual mnemonic device of sorts, to honor not Aristotle's two but three more equal divisions of time which is how most of us track it, from the Greek, that story of three sisters, the Fates who actually predate the gods, the so-called "daughters of necessity" who handle the spindle of Fate, one of them Clotho of that *now,* the Present, who spins the thread of life. Her costars are Lachesis who allots it, as Past, and Atropos who, yes, will cut, tie it off howbeit in some close or faraway Future. And virtually every culture, every language in the world ekes out its tenses from such a triple breakdown—past, present, future—and most to finer distinctions, often via what is deeply structural—verb endings, shifts of case or mood, word order and reorder.

Beyond that, more flexible but equally effective strategies change completely where we thought we were, here or years ago: the use of adverb, adjective, the smallest sound dropped or divided, or something as simple as it is ingenious, as in American Sign Language, the right hand in an abrupt gesture back, over the shoulder to deepen years to decades to centuries, to say *not now, I mean it's already happened.* "Degrees of Remoteness," linguists call what our verbs enact—*zeit worten,* time words, as the Germans say. Because verbs do guide the way we see context, gain perspective and, on the widest canvas, figure how close or far our childhood might be, or the fall of Rome, or the next crucial grocery run, or our death out there somewhere in the vast "not-yet."

Verbs do that. Of course. But where they slip and turn, past to present or to some timeless place between, that inside-out, practically to shine in the dark—isn't that exactly where we feel the great give and stir in poems? Not quite like the very old who lose focus, my husband's grandmother at 102, for example, asking again about Evelyn and Ruth, and his calming her: they're fine, fine, though one had been dead some forty years. She remembers everything, he told me later, it's just that it's happening *all at once.* So, no, not like that, those quiet emphatic bits in poems because perspective kicks in to steady and make shape. Still, it was Augustine who knew the power of the immediate in all this. "If the future and past do exist, I want to know where they are," he wrote in his *Confessions*: "wherever they are, they are not there as future or past, but as present . . . it is only by being present that they *are.*"

Being *present*: you find that, just to be there at all. Boland's poem is no exception. In deeply lyric contemporary work, ones sees this a lot, a memory relived so urgently that the *was* morphs into *is*, at times right from the start. We understand we've entered something like dream though the move is one of acute attention, and often elegiac. The eternal present rears up; can we call it a tense? Probably not. But one poem almost completely darkened by it is "After the Big Storm," arguably one of William Stafford's greatest hits and often anthologized, perhaps written as he claimed most were, in the early morning before anyone else woke. It's set in direct address and from the first line familiar and lived, its "you" cast as friend or acquaintance from adolescence, not the generalized presumptive *you*, the sort of "royal you" one sees so often. "You are famous in my mind," Stafford begins, as straight-up as Boland in her first line.

> When anyone mentions your name
> all the boxes marked "1930s"
> fall off the shelves;
> and orators on the fourth of July
> all begin shouting again.
> The audience of our high school commencement
> begin to look out of the window at the big storm.

Tuned to the past so presently by its verbs, the poem needs a specific event—here it's the graduation—to mark time, and we're lucky to have an image to manage that too, those dated boxes knocked off their shelves, a fairly surreal move for Stafford. A situation this public—even in memory—forces what's thought and said into privacy; more, it's threatened and made smaller by weather, so they seem a deeper secret, these words to the "you" that we happen to overhear.

But this is mere overture, however expertly done. It's the second and third stanzas that narrow the lens, the experience more personal though still public—a real stage recalled, voices there, bits of some lost melodramatic script. "And I think of you in our play— " the speaker says, "oh, helpless and lonely! crying / and your father is dead again. / He was drunk; he fell." Note how the shift to past tense, its one full instance in the piece—he *was* drunk, he fell—makes a sudden backdrop, a gravity, especially given the preceding word "again." Yet this too is overture to the most moving passage coming next that will close the poem, things heard and spoken, the reach across time to startle and go interior and tender against the fury of the storm. But first, the near repetition of the poem's second line, the *name* heard again, and in that a key to the depth of its hold.

> When they mention your name,
> our houses out there in the wind
> creak again in the storm;
> and I lean from our play, wherever I am,
> to you, quiet at the edge of that town:
> "All the world is blowing away."
> "It is almost daylight."
> "Are you warm?"

This might be a case for the highest accolade, where a poem, Adrienne Rich says somewhere, moves from being merely *about* experience, to become an experience itself. Because something happens here that's almost impossible to track, some visionary blip about time itself and how it can work in language—or in spite of it. I keep half-seeing those most unsettling sculptures, the kind one occasionally finds on gravestones or in museums, the figure rooted, lost in raw stone but part of him emerging, fully formed. "and I lean from our play, wherever I am, / to you, quiet at the edge of that town." But slow this down a moment. Here is the present: "They mention your name." Abruptly though, we're out, *back there* on the prairie, again in that storm. And now—*now*—the speaker "leans" from that faraway play—in the past, yes? No, from *wherever I am*. Which is here, isn't it? Not back but nevertheless *in* that play from years ago because of the great magnetic force of this *you*, "quiet at the edge of that town."

So, in fact, where are we? Still where we started at the mere mention of a name, in the present? Isn't that the future, seen as we're expected to see, from back here, the *now* now, in that town, at that play—that bit of it—eerily re-enacted? What's happened to perspective at this point? It's that ghostly *lean*, the speaker in his long arc, future to past on the sudden nerve of the present where the verbs all pretend to keep this. We *do* think this quick, the speed itself underscoring the range of feeling in the poem. But the self, how small it's become, given such push and pull. And what of the startled, near-whisper of those lines recovered after years, fragments from the play, apparently gotten by heart. Is the world still "blowing away"? Is this past or present or something that comes, to keep coming? Can the future return to haunt as much as or more than the past? Yes and yes and yes. "Are you warm?" the speaker says so urgently in those last weighted stresses. Or remembers he said.

The fear of nostalgia should never become a fear of emotion. The heavy-handed, sentimental aura coming in waves off the guy who stands at the window and thinks sweetly back "to the boy he was" makes him, after all, a cliché, a parody, this hyper-conscious speaker who loves watching himself love that looking back and therefore, if not exactly self-serving, is dangerously faux-heroic or at least a little silly. But it's obvious there are ways to do this with tact and surprise and real edge. In Stafford's poem, the voice is kept to human scale; it's vulnerable though in the turns, the very loose play of time, one feels an oracular lift. And however expansive that passage of time, the self so present at first—"You are famous in *my* mind" after all—seems to drop out, Brunelleschi's head once hugely in the way in that mirror almost vanishes even as the personal voice still controls this. Thus wonder. No, thus *perspective*, though not in any way we expected.

Other poems don't end, they begin at this point of distant intensity, the view closer to that map with its long reach over the city of Florence, seen from some high vista. Carl Phillips' "A Great Noise" for example—very little in it is homespun or eye level. The piece starts with the weighted, stark authority single-stressed words in simple past tense: "Then he died." End stop. "And they said: *Another soul free.*" Two sentences equal two lines that make a stanza. So we get a little white space to recover. But this is a very different canvas than Stafford's—or Boland's for that matter. Fewer images, for one. Mostly statement makes this a poem of meditation, of thought life, less about the watcher's direct experience—though it begins that way—than the watcher's pure amazement as he finds a spot and gets a bead on what comes into sight, things larger than life, beyond personal moment. Such a move is cued quiet and strange early with the decision to put that stanza's last phrase in italics: *Another soul free.* "Which was the wrong way to see it, I thought," the poet continues,

> having been there,
> having lain down beside him until
> his body became rigid with what I believe
> was not the stiffening of death
> but of surprise, the initial
> unbelief of the suddenly ex-slave hearing
> *Rest; let it fall now, this burden.*

One can make much of these last three lines, the jolt and grace of that metaphor, the ex-slave brought into this, and thus history, as wide as it is sobering. However we might register the earlier "I believe" as evidence of an immediate voice, in what the dying man hears from the self or from another in such a moment is a shift we almost don't notice, from past to present tense. And then the shock is—we do. *Rest; let it fall now, this burden.* The line is a hinge in so many ways but the new tense opens the floodgates past human remembering, out of the intimate situation described so sharply and into the rest of the poem with its cool, restrained commentary, seemingly ironic though fully in earnest.

The poem gives itself over then to four long sentences threaded down through its lines to take on what is theological and odd and frightening, pretty much leaving behind the heated human part of this except for brief points of comparison. In the most precise and formal language we learn about the soul the body releases, the weight of the body itself via the number of angels—that would be four—required to lift it, this fact from *The Miraculous Translation of the Body/of Saint Catherine of Alexandria to Sinai.* From there it's only angels the speaker observes, those whose "business is hard labor / the work angels, / you can tell: / the musculature; / the resigned way they wear clothes." The *work* angels! But higher orders of such creatures too, the naked seraphim who are "ever-burning," their wings of special interest: "two to fly with / . . . two at the face to withstand / the impossible winds that / are God; / and a third pair—for modesty, / for the covering / of sex." And "a great noise," the speaker tells us at last, "is said to always / attend them"—a shift to passive voice because really, how can we take this head-on anymore? This noise not anything to do with the wings, nothing we could predict, but somehow part of "what is hot, destructive, / and all devotion / to the highest, brightest star."

Is hot, *is* destructive, and *is* all devotion: casting this ancient and certainly familiar dream of angelic orders into that *eternal* immediate tense brings another quality to the movement. In Phillips' poem, maybe it is "the massive heart of the present" as George Oppen called it. For the fabulous becomes grounded, matter-of-fact, and most *of course, of course,* no end to it, no beginning here in the present tense of 2+2=4 or the world *is* round. On the force of that and however skeptical, we helplessly fall into the idea of some ongoing hereafter. We watch with the same muted fascination as the speaker's. This kind of present tense both releases and contains. Who was or what was—no longer is. But what is beautiful and terrifying—always was. And so vastly impersonal now, traded up into myth thus unlike Stafford though we see—still—his haunted lean *back* which means *all at once.* That is, for a moment. Which is to say *this* moment, or for any and all to come.

In 1838, there was yet another simple experiment in the street that would change the way we see—or remember seeing. In that year, Louis Daguerre set up his camera and shot what was happening one morning in Paris on the Boulevard d'Temple, its traffic of horse-drawn carriages and so many people strolling there. But in studio, when he developed his daguerreotype off the copper plate: my god—the street was empty, all moving things erased as if they never were! Only the dazzling light on each building remained, the intricate detail of window and ledge, of trees and their shadows, and one clear human figure—a man having his shoes shined who had stopped for that, at an angle, his leg slightly raised and held there. In other words, only stillness survived those four or five moments Daguerre burned into his copper plate and kept by whatever evil chemicals that came later. Among others, it was Samuel Morse of telegraph fame who praised this particular daguerreotype. "You cannot imagine," he wrote in a letter to the *New York Observer*, "how exquisite is the fine detail portrayal . . . down to the . . . cracks on the walls of the buildings or the pavement." But anything active, lively on that street, intent on the next step: vanished, just gone. So I imagine the lamest joke began its rounds in Paris: Careful. Don't pull the reins too hard in Daguerre's picture—or yes! a headless horse.

Only stillness lasts. Is that true? Is there a template here? Some lesson? A fact or just a time-bound quirk of nineteenth-century optics and light? I like this story, the brimming street forever stripped to an unsettling quiet. But do we remember that way or mainly that way? Are we constructing our own so-called Memory Theaters, the prized and elaborate art of that before things could be easily written down and printed, like the Greeks did, and so many others on through the Middle Ages, way into the Renaissance at work on their same real imaginary places, theaters certainly, but forums too, and abbeys and gardens and cathedrals, their vast rooms and tiny spaces so keenly built into mind to hold each memory, each in its place. One could walk there in one's head, open a door, a box, a drawer, find a small glade, and there, carefully stored: whatever image vivid and intact, whatever thought or argument desired. Could it be something like that, how we keep memory?

So I began bothering people, as if I carried a battered clipboard, standing there full of my never-to-be scientist self: just how do you recall the past? I asked family and friends, near-strangers. I mean, your grandparents for years on their porch, are they a matter of stills, stop-action shots? Is your cousin back there basically a *movie* of your cousin, his bike heading straight toward the river? And what about that news your sister turned toward the window to tell you the truth for once: is she a blur or slowed, her *not* looking at you? And *self* in there too—or not the self really since we only see *from* there, the self as site, this whatever-we-are impossible to *picture* clearly as separate, as apart from our looking.

Memory straight: how such things made us *come to* and connect, or disconnect. And our refiguring again and again after the fact how any of it happened. In what way *does* memory work? At its core, maybe it is a frozen fossil record, the upturned wing darkened and pinned *as if* in flight, that stone lasting thousands of years. Or it might be closer to Eudora Welty's idea that though the world's claim on us, how we learn it, is "made up of moments," it's "not steady. It's a pulse." However it comes, memory is mostly a matter of image, I assume, and probably very present-*seeming* images; I agree with Augustine on that. The results of my poll were multiple: both. We remember both action and stop-action, people said.

Okay, so the jury's out. But I loved their faces as they argued this, each one of them half-dreaming back—where? to picture what?—just to double check their method. And—full disclosure—I see in stills.

Exactly as Susan Sontag, for one, said most of us can't help but enter our past. Like her recollection of a movie "amounts to an anthology of single shots," so, she went on, "it's the same for one's life. Each memory from one's childhood, or from any period not in the immediate past is like a still photograph rather than a strip of film." But certainly such blurred kinetic moments exist; *brain clips* my brother calls those three- or four-second feeds that show up in endless return—a ball as it's kicked, a face slow to anger, three of us walking in woods, though actually I *see* only those other two and maybe the edge of my hand, and trees of course, the uphill path. For to get anything clearly I do have to stop it—stop!—thus ground it, and keep it. Sontag goes further to a kind of cultural claim. These flashpoints suggest, she says, our "highly developed feel for process and transience" but no clear "beginning, middle and end" that might really nail *story* in our lives. Our preferred form of "understanding" isn't particularly narrative, she tells us, but comes "when things are treated as a slice or piece of something larger, potentially infinite." *Infinite*, she says.

That sense of something larger and uncertain, its spirit half "no longer," half "not yet," surely takes us into poems though these creatures are finite aren't they? They end, and begin somewhere. And each has a speaker, however buried that face in the mirror, however ghostly and dodging notice as the mirror reflects back the great world. Yet how what is realized and recalled makes the leap onto the page, how our sense of past and present is carried and changed through language, all collides to continue, and get stranger. At times poetry's deep associative instinct is so quick. The self that started this grows smaller and smaller as the work itself absorbs and layers and takes over. In his "Statement of Poetics," George Oppen quotes Robert Duncan: "the feeling of presence, not concept" as a kind of guide in the intricate process of writing a poem, a loose thing, not rigid, "a necessity" that opens to the "simultaneous music" one feels, a combination, I gather, of image and statement via those many crucial "modulations" to come. "I try one word and another word," Oppen admits,

> and another word, reverse the sequence, alter the line-endings, a hundred two hundred rewritings, revisions—This is called prosody: how to write a poem. Or rather, how to write *that* poem.

And then: "I'll read a few lines of the poem 'Escape,'" he says.

> love like the shining of rails in the night
> the shining way the way away
> from home arrow in the air
> hat-brim fluttering in the wind as she runs
> forward and it seemed to me so beautiful so beautiful
> the sun-lit air it was no dream all's wild
> out there as we unlikely
> image of love found the way
> away from home.

Here the poet offers the turns, forward and reverse, of the smallest gears that went into making this piece.

Should the word be "seemed"? Or should it be "seems"? Is the past more vivid? Or is the past raised into the present, the past *present* in the present? It is not a matter of syntax alone: the "s" of "seems" brings the line into the present—it seemed to me that the "d" of "seemed" was needed there, whatever the "story," the syntax of the story may be, that stop of the "d" must be there that stop which might be revealment. . . .

. . . *that stop which might be revealment.* . . . Which is to say, the shift into honest-to-god past tense—"it seemed to me so beautiful," Oppen writes of this woman who runs—who *ran* now, the "hat-brim fluttering"—no, it *fluttered.* All presses into trance then, to *stop* the "story," he says, a stop that allows distance, allows the experience to settle, which, I suppose, allows comment upon it. One verb, *seemed,* leads the others to shift on their darkened stems *back*—seemed, *it seemed to me*—the eye on the self now, who watches because he once watched. Is everything doubled then? Long ago, and right now too? A freeze of some kind: the love, the wind, the woman, and a "we" comes into this very present point, a shared vision. Because that "d" there is sudden. Oppen says it's a *stop.* As in *look at this, look!*—a profound "revealment" in that gesture which ironically *makes* story by stopping it, poetry's dual impulse, lyric's moment, and narrative's drive hopelessly entangled. Because "note by note" he says later, "the prosody carries the relation of things and the sequence." But to where, and to what unthinkable, inevitable ending? "these little words," Oppen insists, "'and' and 'but'—the word 'is'— . . . in one's mouth . . . strange as infinity."

That idea again: what is infinite, beyond time where—who cares? Perhaps the self and perspective no longer matter. And emotion, however recollected, in tranquility or by a far more furious method, is so pure now, released to air. So it is I hear my neighbor rake leaves from her sidewalk. I'm in the house; I'm writing. At first—what *is* that?—the *scrape scrape scrape* in the slow silence of a November afternoon. Just the most curious sound between silences, like the cough I hear out there at night and early early morning, both places of utter dark. Her cough, as she lights up what I cannot see, cigarette after cigarette: one sound, then no sound, then that sound again. A sequence? Maybe only one cough in an infinity of coughing, or one time, this scraping. But each *seemed* to empty the world, which is to say, fill and flood one instant of time.

Yesterday, or a sound that keeps coming? I stop it, here, to remember.

Heavy Lifting

*. . . don't pick it up. The law of gravity
is the law of art.*

—Karl Shapiro

Before there's a *thing* at all—fire station, airplane, bicycle,
poem—there's a blueprint of some kind. Before that, a drawing
in a sketchbook—*on the verge of, about to.* That's a beginning, a
way to think toward roof or wing, a turning wheel or something
as quick as metaphor in a poem, wayward device for digression
or *voila!* one thing leading to another as structure makes mean-
ing strange and immediate and possible. And dense perhaps,
the hand with a pencil suddenly filling up the page, a roof turn-
ing into a gable, a wheel linked to a chain and then to another
wheel, or metaphor forgetting a while, for how many stanzas,
that it's *like* anything at all. Of course, I'm already stymied at this
X-marks-the-spot, already lifting too much. It's too heavy. "Every-
thing is made out of everything," Leonardo da Vinci records in
his journal in what must be half praise, half exhaustion. So say
this *thing* is a poem. I have to get smaller, down to the simplest
definition. A poem is a box, then; see it in that sketchbook? In
the hovering blue of that blueprint? A poem is a box, a *thing*, to
put other things in.

For safekeeping. Okay. Or it's a time capsule, or even a cata-
pult, for poets with more public ambitions, overarching, or just
arching enough. (Sorry, there it goes, getting bigger . . .) So
again: as a box, the poem *contains.* As a box, it is carried place
to place. And closes. And has secrets. And can weigh quite a
bit. You pack and repack it languidly or with exact, hurried in-
tention. Or with hopeful indifference (back up, see *languidly*
again, and float there with a little more gravity). You forget to

include your favorite things in that poem, or you don't forget to forget, on purpose, putting old habits of beauty aside each time. Maybe it has to be new and sound different. It still weighs a lot. You can hardly lift it to the table, the porch, the car. But the truth is, you can always open the box. You can always look down into it, and take things out, and rearrange its not-at-all-like-little-furniture in there, the whole time lifting it, about to lift. Because the poem is lighter now; it's going up. And now, it *is* up and out of your hands. You can hardly make it out up there, but you know the shape of its shadow down here where we live. It darkens the ground.

I need that darkness first because that's the happy outcome and perhaps the demanding, default position, start or finish. Let's face it: a poem matters because it's about eternal things—death, love, knowledge, time—however these are disguised. The great subjects are endless, never used up. But each waits there in shade. Each weighs at least four thousand pounds. Too much. It's awful, really. How can we stand it? Such melodrama could be—is!—off stage, pacing in the wings, heavy-handed moves ready to prove a point, certain half-seconds clenching up as if underscored three times with a thick black pencil. Maybe. But at times it's so believable, up there in the air. It's impossible, isn't it? Getting such mysterious, monstrous things to lift and keep going? Question: how the hell to do that? "There is no art to flying," said Wilbur Wright, "only the *problem* of flying."

So there are ways, I suppose. Or maybe, for starters, it really is a matter of birdseed, Thomas Edison as a boy convincing another boy that eating a handful or two would make him smart about it all. He'd abruptly know *how* and would launch himself right out the window into perfect flight. *Come on, just a few!* I imagine Edison telling that kid, thinking like a wise guy, but scared a little, past that, almost believing himself. And is it that simple, the old certainty that poems beget poems, something I've heard and absorbed and insisted for others, for years? We read all our lives toward poems we wish to write: black oil sunflower Dickinson and Bishop, thistle seed Hopkins and Whitman, the hard suet of Jeffers or Larkin or Weldon Kees or Plath. That work humbles and empowers, two things at once. Then at the window, looking down to our own city and mountain and farmland, to personal grief, into our own wonder about anything—this hesitation, this screwing up of courage, forgetting for a moment that we've eaten at all. Because our own hunger is crucial too.

But crucial to what in poems? Their dark? Their light? What presses down, or lifts up? Or in Leonardo's terms, is it related to *weight*, this thing that is "corporal" and "changes its position unwillingly," is stable and stays with us, and lasts forever? Or is our hunger something he calls *force*, which is terrible and angelic, utterly "spiritual," he writes, the "true seed in sentient bodies," its energy always a "violence," *fortuitous* and *transforming* and *fleeting*? It desires only "flight from itself." And "death," he adds. This "force" that "willingly consumes itself. . . . From small beginnings, it slowly becomes larger, a dreadful marvelous power.

Open any book about flying, and one reads first about *angle.* Of wing, yes, but the ascent *into* and *up*—the "angle of attack," pilots call it—and *downwards* eventually, even that cautionary no-doubt-about-it *sideways*, almost idling, just living a life for most of the journey. On the instrument panel, that airborne dashboard, so many small, important-looking faces loom up, clocking altitude then "heading," the direction you thought you were going. Then the "turn and slip" device to balance, to stay put or at least level by the old-fashioned charm of needle and ball; certainly the straight ahead speed, the vertical speed, each has its own dial and is busy. You can get such a thing in a kit these days, for as little as ten grand to do a whole airplane in wood or metal, or *composite* which is strictly man-made. You can't predict how long it will take, though you can make a W.A.G., a WAG—*a wild ass guess*—says the book I'm reading about such vessels called "homebuilts," all put together, it seems, right down the street in anyone's neighborhood. But how many of those planes lie half finished, for years in how many garages, this minute? I'll venture a WAG: hundreds, maybe thousands. And someone might be walking through the yard now, thinking to turn on the light in there. Someone thinking to do some sanding, some welding, a little work on it; the wing needs to be set in place, just so.

Because the angle focuses everything. The incline, the turn, the deepest human wish: to rise, to get out of bed. Then later, the second great longing, to be dark and descend. We'll never get over those two brothers at Kitty Hawk, the hard sand there autumn after autumn into winter, four years of failure and half-failure, those Wright boys from Dayton, so far across the country, men who never married, self-taught mechanics and bicycle builders, their hunger large and dogged as their patience. In the old photographic stills, one is running, the other so careful about balance, shifting his weight in *their* homebuilt, a glider, then a motorized glider aloft one day in 1903, four flights' worth, those twelve, thirteen, then fifteen, then the famous fifty-nine seconds, an honest-to-god off the ground moving through space, on its own. But so ingenious, that they angled the wing by way of the bird, by way of its delicate, steely wise hollow-boned pressure.

And poetry? That remains to be seen, but angling up like that, oddly lighter than air, it alters what one sees and *is*—looking down and across now, listening for something else which might resemble the silent largely selfless focus right before any poem kicks in. "Something, somebody, is trying to speak through me," Adrian Stoutenberg begins her "Séance," already in a forward pitch through patient guesswork.

> Ant or ape or a great grandmother,
> perhaps a voice even older,
> perhaps the sea, perhaps a throat in the sea.
> perhaps a shape without eyes or thumbs,
> dust maybe.

To such an eye, by way of such distance, all can seem altered, multiple, and odd. *Everything is made of everything.* But there are rhythms and patterns and all starts simply, with one word or two or three. But—*news flash, key point*—this "lift" engineers talk about, the way air pushed down by the wing's slant must push up and up, it's physics, it's Newton's third law of motion—"for every action, an equal and opposite reaction," and thus the rise, this heavy thing lighter, abruptly, into air. But what force pushes down in a poem? Which in turn, turns furious, pushing up?

"Sundays too my father got up early." So Robert Hayden begins his well-known poem, "Those Winter Sundays" with something remembered, pretty large and already underway. *Sundays too*, he says, as if we know about the other days, the boy, this son listening from a nearby room, from half-dream perhaps to his father's daily ritual in "the blueblack cold" as he fires up the stove to heat the house. *Already underway*: you can hear that lift in the cool assertion about this supposed day of rest—"Sundays too"—no commas for the natural pauses after "Sundays" and "too," the *of course of course* of statement pushing here, this heavy thing, habit, made lighter by its seemingly automatic again-and-again. We are stopped, nevertheless, by the emphatic semi-inversion, a press downward on the wing—flying directly now *into* the wind for greater lift—with that structural decision to put the day first, in that clipped near-shorthand way, a trochee here, the poem launched on that initial no-doubt-about-it heavy stress. After all, it's not "On Sundays, my father got up early," the graceful rise of a more iambic beginning, and definitely not the prosaic "My father got up early on Sundays." This is fierce. There's strain in the phrasing—"Sundays too"—a resistance that releases, one line later, the lingering, triple-weighted "blueblack cold," this "blueblack" suddenly older than anything we've thought about for a while, the two words flush against each other, as a *kenning* works right of out of *Beowulf*, its "cold" flooding father, son, memory itself.

It's the final two lines of this poem that show its true mettle, though one can't praise enough how this steady unsonnet sonnet moves toward that closure, accounting for the father's predawn labors—his cracked and aching hands, his polishing of shoes—but Hayden is never sentimental. From the start, the harder truths—including the boy who speaks "indifferently" to this father—are not airbrushed out.

> I'd wake to hear the wild splintering, breaking.
> When the rooms were warm, he'd call
> and slowly I would rise and dress,
> fearing the chronic angers of that house.

And so on, to the well-known ending of this poem that takes those hard truths and weighs them so hopelessly—"What did I know, what did I know / Of love's austere and lonely offices?"—

lines often recited, committed to memory, and for good reason; they stand by themselves. And maybe it's natural to cherish them. I'm remembering again, years ago in Indianapolis, a car making its way through snowy streets, a handful of us in there, shouting out those two lines. And again, in a friend's kitchen two states away, our saying out those lines in the air. They keep doing that, coming back. And maybe not *why*—that's a matter for more private places—but how exactly? The given, bony rise in any question—the open, wondering built-in aerial view offered by that particular sentence structure—immediately gives these lines their initial internal power, and the repetition too, so by its second utterance—"What did I know, *what did I know*"—all is rattled and urgent, secret really, this speaker fully unto himself now. And what do we catch there, past lament? He stares again into that lost flash of childhood: "what did I know / Of love's austere and lonely offices?" One word, or two. So a poem starts, and finishes. *Austere* has to have one of the most violently beautiful effects in English, distant and vulnerable at once, public and hidden, held upright by enormous pressure inside and out. And here, its sound—its iambic lift—the second syllable stressed adds a brief and expansive counterrhythm. We hear in that both contraction and expansion.

But it's *offices* that compels and is brilliant, a word going straight into ancient practice. I remember a young priest in my childhood parish at dawn, reading the *matins* from his Divine Office, walking the streets as he read, never looking up as we biked by to early Mass. Something vast, nearly incomprehensible looms up in that word. In Hayden's poem, it brings humility; what's been done is done again; one merely partakes of that. But nobility's there too; ditto, done and done, this time into tradition so heavy, we no longer even know how to weigh it. The power of a single word can be staggering. And finding it, trying to figure out why it works—really why other choices do not—can take a long time and is the writer's most essential, brain-fracturing job. After all, a poem is a box to put things in, and with that comes the task of taking things out, then it's all over again, putting the radiant things, however dark they are, back in. Which is to say, in my friend's kitchen that summer, we gratefully remembered the poem, singing out those last two lines. And *offices*—I blurted out as any Catholic would, even one as long-lapsed as I am. That's great in there, isn't it? *Offices!* I mean, what if—here's a terrible thought—what if he had written *promises* instead? "love's austere and lonely *promises*"? And my friend agreed, her face suddenly screwed up in that funny gag-me way, her index finger already miming that halfway-down-the-throat thing.

Because "promises" *is* awful for about a half dozen reasons. Which, of course, makes at least that number of ways to prove "offices" so remarkable here. But it's not a matter of meter really, since both words are dactyls, three syllables whose first comes down hard before moving forward unstressed, first emphatic then that suggestion of *falling*, "a descent" Paul Fussell calls it, the critic who has written with such smart crankiness about these things. This downward move is especially dramatic against the *rising* shape—and hopeful, one might read that—of the line's earlier words, *austere* itself and "*love's*"—no—*Of love's*, both iambic moves, stepping lightly *up*, into the stressed second syllable. Or if you hear a spondee there—two equal beats, *Of love's*—it only deepens the gravity, those two beats stretching time, Fussell's claim for that particular rhythm, suggesting weariness, he says, or fullness. But the words *promises* or *offices* are metrically similar; the difference in their power must lie elsewhere, maybe in what a pilot considers, the four elements that keep any plane going: lift and weight, thrust and drag. So the airborne wish, sometimes for thousands of miles.

Mileage—and certainly altitude—in a poem is harder to gauge, though one can start any first line in Seattle and land in Chicago or Philadelphia, most likely the same day. And—considering metrics again—think of the downward press, that first syllable's trochaic/dactylic hit that colors the very end and beginning of this poem, lifting and darkening in near equal amounts. Drag, though, is an aerodynamic force that resists the object as it moves through a fluid, which both air and water are, and which, I'd argue for a long time, thought is too—a fluid, a near-viscous dream. To land in any of these, one needs drag, which is to say, the plane routinely drops down its lumbering wheels not only to soften the impact but simply to add a needed baseline trouble, to get heavier and bigger at closure, thus to slow this last possible moment of the journey.

60

Words themselves drag behind them plenty of history, numerous other identities brought to the mix. And poets worry everything from the start. So back to *promises* vs. *offices*. At first glance, the former has, well, promise. Anyone might *promise* a lot or a little: to pick up ice cream and avocadoes at Pay Less, to stop the mail for a few days, to make dinner, to keep a secret, to stay married. But the word can feel coy, even precious, especially following any reference to love, as it would in Hayden's poem if we forced our bad revision. A shaky choice—*promises*—and pretty much predictable, evoking the classic June-wedding froth or worse, that pink icing turning petulant á la *but you made a promise*, says Tiffany to Chad (or Ryan or Trevor), wringing her hands in *Days of Our Lives* or *The Guiding Light* (my mother's favorite, but perhaps long off the air). So melodrama is more than a suggestion of danger. With certain words, like *fraught*, it's fraught with it, too willfully weighted, too much drag, I suppose, and not enough thrust to keep going, however right and graceful it is to hesitate here at the end of Hayden's poem where threat is genuine. Because there's already so much *falling* buried in those key words and—double whammy—closure itself supplies a natural big bang and weight written right into the contract of the "meter making argument" that Emerson claimed a decent poem always has to be. In short, word choice is a tricky business. Such endless shifting Orville Wright needed at first, his body this way and that, to fly that delicate vessel! One needs drag, but not too much; thrust, but of a certain kind. It must surprise, however small that messing now with the angle of the wing to bring it all down, and in. Where it continues its haunting.

Offices then—because at heart, that word hasn't quite the heavy-handed personal confinement that "promises" does, ticking off and getting (*look-at-me!*) credit for its duty-bound minutes and hours. Instead, "offices" goes back and back, past counting, almost courtly in its historical reserve, and will go on without, even in spite of us, thank you very much, though not so very much. That's the lonely part, in part (*lonely*, yet another word with a first syllable stress in this line, its second syllables unstressed, just a shade or two going under, so Fussell might declare it all the more dark, the descent even steeper). Thus this poem, this large shuttering machine. is tiny, intricate—only fourteen lines!—coming to a sudden, howbeit still moving stop.

In Leonardo's journals, you can find many curious pages on flight. "I have divided the 'Treatise on Birds' into four books," he writes, this treatise not strictly on birds (though a great deal of it is wing work: flapping vs. gliding, taking off, coming down). He eventually gets to bats and fishes, flying machines of course and famously (their linen and sinew and pulleys, the staring figure drawn seated in the center between sticks and rope), then into the straight and intricate mechanics where many of us might blur, glaze over. Always though, "the heaviest part will become the guide of the movement." So watch out, I suppose, where exactly you put that part.

In the litany, one of our oldest literary shapes, *where*, and even *when* seems hardly a choice, that "heaviest part" just there at the start of each line and after that, it's like the astronauts' floating-through-air, their arms and legs flailing as they speed far away from gravity's pull. Thus one more of Leonardo's dictums on flight: "Those feathers . . . farthest away from their points of attachment will be the most flexible." I read *flexible* here as lighter, as more subtle, as the variation Ezra Pound claimed every form needs to escape its essential fixed point, though it's exactly that shifting, back and forth, that makes art. "Repetition makes us feel secure," Robert Hass has written, "and variation makes us feel free." And it's hard not to think first of Whitman in this context, his reverence for and brilliance at these two sides of litany pushing out, then back in his *Leaves of Grass*, each line a miniature of the whole trip, keeping a kind of sweet stall through an initial repeating phrase as the poem pushes forward.

But I'm not considering an overall habit. I'm thinking *mid-poem* really, *mid-flight* where so much of the journey takes place. Which is to say for a moment I'm trading Whitman for T. S. Eliot, two you'd never find in the same bomb shelter, though both would be alert and wary enough there, counting down water jugs and cans of beans to the last hunger and thirst ahead. In Eliot's "Four Quartets," the second one, the "East Coker" section, litany comes in abruptly, a surprise, not the given instrument it is for Whitman. It's a way for Eliot, already aloft, already up there, to hover soundlessly and still make noise. And because this is Eliot, we enter *big*, through pure incantation: "O dark dark dark," he writes, "they all go into the dark." And so we have our *anaphora*, the repeated word in any litany, the fixed point to which at least some of those flexible tip-of-the-feather moves will return. What's surprising in this section is how flexible those feathers are. Eliot is looser in one way than Whitman. The compulsion to return to that *dark* and *dark* is not so demanding, not the default setting every time as Whitman might do it. Eliot doesn't load the line *as line* so meticulously. And what's swallowed by this dark? Everyone, all, i.e.:

> The captains, merchant bankers, eminent men of letters,
> The generous patrons of art, the statesmen and the rulers,
> Distinguished civil servants, chairmen of many committees,
> Industrial lords and petty contractors, all go into the dark,
> And dark the Sun and Moon, and the Almanach de Gotha
> And the Stock Exchange Gazette, the Directory of Directors.

The accumulation here jumps categories, large groups of people, then how vast it gets with "Sun and Moon," then back to its daily inch by inch with "the Stock Exchange Gazette." Eliot's human beings are cast by where they work, high and low, and are far more generalized than Whitman's, where a prostitute, say, has accessories and "draggles her shawl" as his sign painter carefully letters "in blue and gold." Still, the more specific Eliot gets, the more he simply *moves*—and the less he's characteristically ponderous. We get a little air, some release and sideways flight in that rapid but squarely paced shifting, that piling-up before it all goes "into the dark and dark" and finally into the "moment of darkness on darkness."

Eliot does something else to lift and hover. Suddenly *cold* takes over *dark* in that cadence; "and cold the sense," he writes. Then *lost* too, "and lost the motive for action." Steady, steady, we even rise on that move, a change in the repeat of *dark*—now this *cold*, this *lost*, a break in the weather, a new kind of breathing, more urgent. We're upright, still gliding, before Eliot drops completely out of litany and into *story* as poets sometimes tend to it, on an extended image working sideways, both to draw a moment out of human time and to make metaphor. He evokes the theater first, whose backdrop scenes go up, then vanish nightly, their "distant panorama" of "hills and trees" all "rolled away," and then his next great passage, where all disappears in the "underground train," London's subway, the tube, that fabled site of so much longing and symbol for this poet. There they sit, the city's blank staring citizens, and "behind every face" the "growing terror of nothing to think about." Of course, we descend in the weight of that image. This is Eliot, after all, whose genius loved most the dark default. In the meantime, though, we were orbiting a little and had that vision, looking with such sweep at everyone, and by inference at ourselves, so busy and doomed even now.

In fact, more ways exist to stay aloft, another set of *creature* ways to manage that. I know Leonardo was obsessed with birds, and stared them through. And the Wright brothers too kept watching gulls, taking notes, reportedly flapping their own arms bent at elbow and wrist; no, it was buzzards and gannets at Kitty Hawk that swooped and dove. But at Berkeley, not long ago, biologists glommed onto a less in-your-face flyer. They've made a very high tech mini-robot, a giant gnat, a fruit fly, really—calling it a "robofly"—to see how the smallest of animals do it, stay up there, minus the powerful wings of falcon or owl. Insect strategies are many, here, one of their first techniques—the so-called "delayed stall" where tiny wings dash forward and up (something neither bird nor plane can do), the fiercest angle. And how fast? Very fast, but Robofly is slower and larger; the human eye can see it.

And would Philip Larkin mind the thought of certain moves in his "Sad Steps" flush up against such an airborne feat? His poem, which initially moves off a sixteenth-century sonnet from Sir Philip Sidney's "Astrophel and Stella" and that poet's own "sad steps" that evoke the moon, quickly becomes Larkin's own night-bound invention. I'm counting out his six tercets, three movements really, on one of the great subjects—time (our getting old, our looking back, our right here, right now, our way of going back and forth), not to mention the other perennial moments here—the early hour sky or how anyone might rise midway through sleep to pee. In this shift of high to low, sacred to profane, there's humor, its automatic buzz and rise. Thus we know at once we're reading Larkin, not Eliot, not even Whitman. So maybe Robofly is semi-proper, a way of paying homage. Larkin first gives us time and place. "Groping back to bed after a piss," he writes,

> I part thick curtains, and am startled by
> The rapid clouds, the moon's cleanliness.
>
> Four o'clock: wedge-shadowed gardens lie
> Under a cavernous, a wind-picked sky.
> There's something laughable about this.

Is this what anyone might see? The moon's up there, and clouds like "cannon smoke," and "roofs below." And heavy, clean, this stall, that won't let that moon go, this staring that keeps it coming (wings cutting forward, a steep then steeper angle) in Larkin's pronouncements:

> High and preposterous and separate—
> Lozenge of love! Medallion of art!
> O wolves of memory! Immensements!

That sudden angle, this "delayed stall," is mimed hard by the fragmentation here, more, by his precise jabs at definition, how-be-they wild and tongue-in-cheek. Real or imagined, it's still triumphant. Exclamation points, count them: four! They push everything higher, lighter. And the simple repetition—"of love. . . . of art. . . . of memory. (Knock on wood: here's the heft of litany again though shrunk down and in its locket.) That *of* and *of* and *of* cuts up at an urgent angle however playful. (Can you see that intricate fuzzy wired creature—moon or fruit fly or poem—hovering there? And so much bigger for it?) Such high invention to make real that moon, before the *no* comes, and "one shivers slightly, looking up there," the poet now dropping abruptly to a more level tone, shifting from his mock heroics to something more felt and nagging about this moon. Which is to say, worlds sadder.

The hardness and the brightness and the plain
Far-reaching singleness of that wide stare

Is a reminder of the strength and pain
Of being young; that it can't come again,
But is for others undiminished somewhere.

In writing once about Auden, Larkin linked the words "funny" and "dreadful"—*dreadful* in its first straightforward meaning, i.e., full of genuine dread. "High and preposterous," Larkin reminds us in his own poem, this "lozenge of love" calling up the "wolves of memory" and so many "immensements," none of which will "come again." So humor finds its weight in such an unlikely mix, and so that darker weight finds lift, fracturing itself *endurable*, even radiant for a moment. We find ourselves looking down and up and past that moon and its usual guises now, into a very different—and unsettling—expanse.

In the history of flight, there are thousands of stories, and quite a few belong to the Wright brothers, though one is legendary, coming out of their bicycle shop in Dayton, Ohio. Two elements are memorable: an empty inner tube box, and Wilbur Wright leaning in the doorway, talking idly to a customer not too long after the last century turned. I see him there. He's picked up the box. He's fiddling with it; it must feel good in his hands as he keeps talking, listening, nodding his head, turning the cardboard this way and that. Then he's looking down. No, he's *more* than looking down. How this simple movement—his twisting the box—superimposed itself on the rigid wing of their not-yet-flying machine shows metaphor in its most heightened—and practical—moment. *What thing is shaped as this thing is shaped?* That's William Carlos Williams decades later, from his poem "Asphodel, that Greeny Flower," a question I've loved too much, and quoted too often, but it narrows to an absolute in poetic thinking: we learn by the leap, the comparison, the analogy; two unlikely things together make a third thing, and so we move forward. *A wing could do this*, Wilbur Wright must have thought, maybe vaguely at first, but more and more, it must have taken hold under the talk-talk about whatever, the storm last night, or the new brick work going in to make East Third a wider street, this deeper kind of mulling-over that runs on and on under the surface fact, almost by itself, the sort of lucky thing that *comes to us*, these glimpses. So poems are twisted too, drifting there, in progress regardless, kept alive even when those who write them are distracted, not particularly honed to the task.

As for aviation, Wright's fiddling that day was the key to "wing warping," the brothers' name for this great gift and innovation so simple really, to solve the problem of control, their craft now too heavy and past the point one of them piloting could merely shift his weight left, right, forward, backward to *will* the plane through air and so avoid disaster. The Wrights' sketch and blueprint of the design was stunning. In it we see the beauty of pure form. And the plane itself seems almost whimsical now, the wings' edges made bendable by runs of two bicycle chains jury-rigged to a couple of levers. But the point is this: what seemed forever rigid to everyone—the airplane wing—was not. And the larger point: was it really possible? Yes. We would fly.

To warp something then. To make flexible what all along was kept as *rule*, committed in the mind to stone: the very thought, even in theory, is a great relief, a lightening of both inside and outside pressure. Applied to poetry, sometimes it's dramatic, such warping, denoting a sea change in a poet's work, John Berryman's say, his messy and vernacular move to the *Dreamsongs* from a more formal habit in *Homage to Mistress Bradstreet* or his *Sonnets*, a twisting of that inner tube box, a serious wing-warp. And the nature of that particular flight, its drag and thrust? its lift and weight? "A creepy, scorching book," Adrienne Rich wrote, reviewing it for *The Nation*. "He uses any conceivable tone of voice and manner to needle, wheedle, singe, disarm and scarify the reader." Can you see Orville Wright up there at his levers? The bicycle chain angling the wing just barely, tragedy averted by a couple of degrees. No crash this time. Not yet.

Because tragedy is all over the *Dreamsongs*, its threat presses down on every line. Which is why, perhaps, we think of the deep play in these poems as a kind of resistance, Newton's counter-motion coming up by way of Berryman's comic brilliance. It's Larkin again, mixing dark and light, thrust and drag, to keep aloft and believable. "Life, friends, is boring," Berryman announces straight away in Dreamsong 14. "We must not say so." But some of the pieces are less stagy, just painfully wry or simply edgy, which is a balancing too. Number 29 is an example of this, taking on one of poetry's great subjects—regret, guilt, remorse—three curses of memory that make one curse in the poem. With characteristic dark grace line to line, this poet twists and warps and finally convinces. Note the music here. Note Berryman's feel for a big-voice but tentative sound, a point/counterpoint managed by inversion, fable, surprise, omission.

> There sat down, once, a thing in Henry's heart
> so heavy, if he had a hundred years
> & more, & weeping, sleepless, in all them time
> Henry could not make good.
> Starts again always in Henry's ears
> the little cough somewhere, an odour, a chime.

How huge, then small this begins—*There sat down, once*—the cadence so familiar, as if this were the oldest story we have to tell. But where? In "Henry's heart" and so this very public utterance turns personal, private and "so heavy," this *thing*—too horrible to be named—and to prove that weight, a kind of piling up, years of this thing, "& more, & weeping, sleepless, in all them time." This could be pure melodrama so easily, but it's rushed, its shutter speed so fast, even tiny decisions—quick! screw up the grammar, go slipperier, enjamb! enjamb! or use an ampersand, not the proper "and"—to loosen, to lighten before the line break quiets everything for a second, then the fall via so many hard single stresses: "Henry could not make good." So we're down—it's Fussell's lamenting spondee again—and seriously end-stopped. Which is to say, real pause. Silence. Until—"Starts again always in Henry's ears / the little cough somewhere, an odour, a chime." This is a large measure of Berryman's power, his willingness to move. His rapid juxtaposition makes weighty complexity here almost lace-like, delicate. Where to go? To the triggering agents, these bad charms—a cough, an odour, a chime—to bring this *thing* back.

His sleight of hand continues, this expert shifting. It's Berryman's hairpin control of tone. Its wing warp takes us through time, his flashing in reverse to Italian sculpture in the next stanza, its profile's thousand-year look of reproach unchanged. Next, it's the very clipped, the fragment, "(A)ll the bells:"—a colon placed after "bells," Berryman forcing an equation: "too late," he says. Under such a load, there's only retreat. "This is not for tears; / thinking." Then "but"—that word of sweet suspension, signal for every reverse turn, rise, second thought.

> But never did Henry, as he thought he did,
> end anyone and hack her body up
> and hide the pieces where they may be found.
> He knows: he went over everyone, & nobody's missing.
> Often he reckons, in the dawn, them up.
> Nobody is ever missing.

Juxtaposition, the bendable wing—we're up, then down—a long sentence undercut quick by a shorter one. Or the surprise of the misplaced prepositional phrase, severing a warmer, more expected rhythm: "Often he reckons, in the dawn, them up," a kind of startle, a small awkward leap in the line before the repeated phrase here, going quieter for that. *Nobody is ever missing.* Violence cast into dream and bewilderment by metaphor—that third thing—in the secret half light that metaphor always is. And it's a draw now, the day just beginning, night still hanging on.

Leonardo's notion that "the heaviest part will become the guide of the movement" seems reasonable, but is it? Certainly we feel for that weight as we write, writing toward it, at least our side vision alert for it. After all, gravity is one of the three basic forces on earth, the earth itself its center because—I quote chemist Robert Wolke here—"the more mass a body has—the more particles of matter it contains—the stronger its aggregate attractive force would be. That's why," he points out, "when you jump off a ladder, earth doesn't fall upward to meet you." This is maybe the best argument I've seen for work whose center of gravity and focus is the world and not the self. We know that ladder, after all. We've fallen off many a time. Because it's the mysterious *other* out there that pulls us to itself. But this perhaps is another matter.

All along there's that deeper Leonardo thing, weight vs. force, *weight* so stable and unchanging, those unwieldy subjects of poetry, for instance—love, death, knowledge, time—and *force* working through that weight, a more wily spirit out and about, "in flight" and "transforming," terrible and angelic both. The voice in a poem seems also to transform, to do this give and take, drawing itself through the heaviest part, though often, and often effectively, it's not straight on, not an easy matter of calling up the lowest chords out of string section to make sense of the speechless moment *after* the car crash in some overwrought made-for-TV movie. Such a force, this voice, works more powerfully much of the time by inference, a sort of ruse, where we look away for a second, pretend *this terrible thing is not the point, not really.* Though it is. And I may be half-eyeing Larkin again, and perhaps Berryman in this since irony and outright humor work this sideways way. In either case, Leonardo's *force* becomes a lifting device to get whatever overwhelming ache and baggage across, making it less, not more, so less *is* more. And then we're impossibly up there, in flight.

I don't know exactly how to approach what Emily Dickinson did with her "flood subject," one of the great ones, death, which was everywhere in 1862 when she wrote so much, the Civil War upping the bloody count daily. Leonardo's weight here is surely in that fact, the end in store for all of us, a stable, immoveable element if there ever was one. But Dickinson, like Larkin and Berryman, is distracted, and in her best work refuses to belabor the obvious in any ponderous, expected way. There's her much-cited and unbelievably odd take on the deathbed scene, poem #465, with its fly—its *fly!*—as the key figure, its "Blue—uncertain stumbling Buzz—" that comes between the dying speaker and the light, until the windows *fail*, a run of image that would almost be whimsical if it weren't so dark.

Such oddity—if not comic, at least surreal—works because it isn't quite satire, which is to say, the speaker isn't grandstanding, isn't holding forth or looking down. That's not the *force* that makes this so chillingly accurate. When asked about his own use of humor during an interview with Robert Phillips of the *Paris Review*, Larkin was clear about the distinction: "to be satiric, you have to think you know more than anyone else. I've never done that."

Not knowing more, perhaps, but not responding to certain things in the same old, same old as everyone else: that might be the key, this force that Leonardo relished, a matter of surprise and angle. Which is to say, be just a little *off*—the bendable wing again—and so deflect. And invent something called flight. In Dickinson's poem #467, what's going on seems, at first anyway, less dramatic. "We do not play on Graves," she begins, this *we* apparently a group of children, and this speaker the self-appointed leader of the group. The voice continues in that most super-rational, reasonable way that such children often have.

> Because there isn't Room—
> Besides—it isn't even—it slants
> And People come—
>
> And put a Flower on it—
> And hang their faces so—
> We're fearing that their Hearts will drop—
> And crush our pretty play—

One can see instantly how this vessel stays in the air—pure pretending, a ruse because surely the heaviest part of the poem cries out not so secretly: *this is a grave, damn it. Dead people live here. We'll all get this address sooner or later.* But Dickinson's pilot turns this so patiently, laying out reasons through the earnest explanation of a child impatient with the clueless adult who must stand there listening. "Besides—it isn't even—it slants" we overhear. Such grounded certainty in the language, so painfully missing the point, which is the point, of course. But it's so like Dickinson to tweak the darker vein here eventually. And maybe the dead speak like this too. Thus we land, drawn back to the most dire fact, a more adult shadow suddenly on the language. And yes, back to Leonardo's heaviest part.

> And so we move as far
> As Enemies—away—a

> Just looking round to see how far
> It is—occasionally—

It's that one last look, that "occasionally," that reweights—and lifts—every word here. As if we could forgot what poetry is really about.

O'Connor plus Bishop
plus Closely plus Distance

Just this: Imagine the phone call Elizabeth Bishop made to Flannery O'Connor from Savannah, Georgia, October 1957. I can picture the details: the poet ringing up the operator to place the call through to Milledgeville; O'Connor's stalwart mother, Regina, with her *Yes, surely, just a minute please*; the walk to her daughter's room in the front of the house where the writer has been working all morning, turning away from her desk toward the window on occasion, her eye out for the peacocks in the yard either roosting or strutting, the males keeping their brilliant secret for now. Bishop continues, phone in hand in a hotel lobby, studying, as she later claimed, "a display of pecans and boxes of 'Miss Sadie's Bourbon *Balis*'" a few hours before her freighter sails for Brazil. About the call, she's tentative: maybe this isn't such a great idea. "I think I'm afraid of Flannery," she confessed in a note to the editor Robert Giroux in 1979, thanking him for the collection of O'Connor's letters he'd just published which "are wonderful, aren't they?" O'Connor was, very simply, "the best of our contemporary prose writers," Bishop insisted in an interview. And early on, admiring the stories, what she considered poetry in them, she admitted she was "green with envy." Later, "intimidated" was the word she used.

I'm with Bishop. These things can so easily flash and morph: the smarts and the fear, or the fear because of the smarts. Nevertheless, Bishop did make that call. And invitations came from both sides, for the poet to visit the farm in Georgia, and O'Connor Brazil, where Bishop lived for years. But the two women never met. A correspondence did flourish, the first exchange some ten months before the poet phoned up, the initial contact—out of the blue really—a fan letter from Bishop short-ly after the publication of *A Good Man Is Hard to Find.* "Please don't feel this requires any answer," the poet wrote. But answer, O'Connor did.

I think it safe to say they had a kind of mutual crush, how-ever remotely played out, their similarities about equal to how much they would never be alike. "I have great respect for your work," O'Connor wrote back to Bishop in an early letter, "though I am almost too ignorant ever to know why I like what I like." And in that same note: "It means considerable to me to know you have read and liked my stories." They seemed—no small thing—to recognize each other, their friend in com-mon Robert Lowell, a companion of Bishop's for years whom O'Connor had met at Yaddo.

As for that phone call, all I'm able to do is listen as Bishop might have listened to Regina O'Connor's footsteps; "the par-ent," her daughter called her in affection and exasperation as the writer's lupus took hold and her reliance on her mother deepened. I imagine a knock on a door, the startle of words in the distance, something about a certain "Miss Bishop" calling from Savannah, and *No, I don't know why.*

The fact is I could stay here forever, in suspended vigil hap-pily going nowhere, picturing one, then the other, two writers I found early, who've meant much to me. O'Connor first, in my late teens, I loved instantly and full blast for her scathing humor, being a secret delinquent myself. Then Bishop, a poet I found in graduate school, not through a class assignment—too early for that (she wasn't really "taught" yet)—but my teacher, James Tate, told me to read her, I'd like her. Which I did—a lot—but it took a while. She seemed slow, so careful, and I was too itchy.

Full disclosure though: as I write this, I'm in another much lower sort of vigil, my knee slowly healing itself painfully anew; cut, replaced by steel and plastic, then brought back together with nearly two dozen stitches, the scar looking like some zip-per with an attitude. No comparison to O'Connor's lot, I real-ize; mine—fingers crossed—is to get better and walk right, my surgeon-inflicted wound savagely minor and really not-much-at-all in the greater scheme. But being down for the count, sunk swollen to ache and throb, is a time-stop. You have to stay put and stare and think, that's all, as someone's no-nonsense grand-mother might say.

"In a sense, sickness is a place more instructive than a long trip to Europe," O'Connor wrote to her friend Betty Hester. And it's true. Pain does take you out, backward and forward. In its freeze I can at least savor this new news to me, that these two writers whose work I cherish did find and admire each another. The past becomes future: what will they say on the phone as I ghost that house at the edge of Milledgeville, my time-traveled forced entry most certainly ill-advised, if not illegal? A passionate lapsed Catholic, I have this weakness: I live in fear of hagiography. I could, however, rearrange the furniture of this imagining, tangle it further by way of an image, a small vignette taken from O'Connor's essay "King of the Birds."

So—say she is distracted at the window as she gathers herself to walk toward the phone. Say one of the peacocks in the yard has just exploded into radiant color, fanning out his great tail squarely in front of a delivery truck come up near the house, stopping that driver cold. O'Connor, too, is spellbound, giving way to laughter. And Elizabeth Bishop, who would have relished such a scene, is waiting on the other end of the line, and she has no idea.

Not that idea had much to do with it, at the start anyway. O'Connor and Bishop were smitten with hard image in the most earnest, physical sense: by way of pencil, brush, and, in O'Connor's case, a sharp knife on linoleum blocks. Drawing mattered to them as personal habit, the actual doing of it. Which means seeing closely at a distance mattered, something that takes time and silence and is, like writing, a lonely art. But no words! You pretty much just look, outward and inward: for the stories, the poems. This rather thrilling fact that both were also visual artists isn't a door but a key to a door that opens up their method.

"Any discipline can help your writing," O'Connor argued in one of her essays, "particularly drawing. . . . The writer should never be ashamed of staring. There is nothing that doesn't require his attention." And about revision, she once advised a friend to write a version of her story in reverse, if only to get a fresh take on it as O'Connor had been urged to do by studying her sketches upside down in drawing class. More ammo: her artist's eye alert to color, O'Connor wrote her friend Maryat Lee that her second (and final) novel, *The Violent Bear It Away*, seemed a thing "gray, bruised-blue and fire-colored," her description admittedly metaphoric but grounded in actual use. Armed with brush and paints kept in a tackle box earned fairly enough through a couple of S&H Green Stamps books, she had been painting regularly for a long time by then, sometimes self-portraits. A tongue-in-cheek favorite? Herself head to head with one of her peafowl, the obsession she had with birds—the weirder the better—a beloved fact about this writer, so much so that later, in an undated letter, Bishop would ask "Don't you have a picture of yourself—and a peacock?"

To go further, though, is to go back. I mean, it's altogether one of those shocking *aha!* moments that O'Connor was, from a young age, a cartoonist. The jolt then shifts to a knowing nod, a certain 2 + 2 = 4 look on anyone I've told this who's read her fiction. Because she always stepped back, her eye earnest and playful. Consider what she liked to recall about herself as a small child: a cameraman from Pathe News, showing up in Savannah to film her prized chicken walking backward, or—according to her biographer, Brad Gooch—her last-minute desperate move to save herself in the high school home economics course she'd been blowing off. A fellow classmate, Barbara Beiswanger, remembers exactly how their teacher, Miss Abercrombie, announced the final exam coming up shortly, all garments made during the quarter to be displayed: "I can hardly see how you are going to get a whole outfit finished and ready, Mary Flannery, by that time," she taunted. Well, ta-da! Not the usual aprons and underwear the other girls managed over the term, O'Connor's outfit sewn in the wee hours for her pet duckling depended on a technical point: nothing said about *human* garments. (P.S. she did pass the course.)

Quirky, yes, and foreshadowing enough. But the regular cartooning she did for school publications, her eye tracking more usual foibles, was serious. In addition, her weekly submission of cartoons during college and beyond—to *The New Yorker*, no less (with, alas, no luck)—makes that ambition even clearer. It's not just the delight in all this that clicks the aha! button in those who treasure this writer. "She gouged out" her drawings on those linoleum blocks with a very sharp tool, O'Connor scholar Bruce Gentry reminded me in an e-mail. You take no prisoners that way, I thought. You cut, you roll the black ink. High contrast. Bodies all over the stage.

As for Bishop, bits keep flashing for me from her late poem "The End of March," which O'Connor never lived to see, where friends walk and walk along the ocean on a dismal late-winter, not-quite-spring day. The scene is awful and nowhere, the flotsam a matter of soaked gobs of string along the beach, the water itself an icy gray on gray. Then her writer's eye—no, her artist's, near-cartoonist's eye—finding her central image so much the way she might have drawn such a thing: slowly, only gradually remembered, questionable wires snaking out of a dune shack weather-beaten sweet to strange. It's a start, a solitary easing back to a most singular Eden. "I wanted to get as far as my proto-dream-house," Bishop wrote,

> my crypto-dream-house, that crooked box
> set up on pilings, shingled green,
> a sort of artichoke of a house, but greener
> (boiled with bicarbonate of soda?) . . .

"A good story," O'Connor claimed, "is literal in the same sense that a child's drawing is literal. When a child draws, he doesn't intend to distort but to set down exactly what he sees, and as his gaze is direct, he sees the lines that create motion. Now the lines of motion that interest the writer are usually invisible." She called these "lines of spiritual motion" and "an action of grace." And there's also what's memorable. Bishop wrote to O'Connor how "strange" it was that just at the "thought" of her stories, everything "popped right back into my head . . . names, whole phrases. I only remember some of Chekov's like that."

So much depends . . . on the right image! Bishop named one of her own watercolors *Interior with Extension Cord*, an unusually playful choice. But the cord itself is absurd. Too long and thick, it climbs the wall, crosscuts the ceiling, runs straight down another wall. Total crazy overkill. All that effort to make the circuit work—but the tiny lamp in question, on a skinny side desk, is equally funny, even its little shade askew. There's a stool, a white bureau. A doorway opens to distant suggestion in its floral wash out there: maybe someone's left in a hurry, or is yet to come. Her comic at-an-angle endears, but it haunts the room. All at once, it's this, too: you're by yourself, you're the only one looking into that place, the mind's eye making all things jerry-built, partial, unnerving. When Flannery O'Connor was working on the novel *Wise Blood*, John Selby, her editor—but not for long—grew impatient with the nine chapters he saw. He fired off a letter of complaint. "You are writing out of the small world of your experience," the book filled with "peculiarity, a kind of aloneness." Annoyed or downright furious, the twenty-five-year-old wrote back. "The quality of the novel I write will derive precisely from peculiarity or aloneness, if you will. . . ."

Just so, I remember an electrician telling me that it's sometimes the wiser choice to allow additional out-of-wall wiring to circle however it can, not always to leave it in expected low-lying places. The thing about Bishop's watercolor is that her extension cord—outrageous and out of reach—demands, as her poems often do, that we also invent a very human backstory: some poor last someone on a ladder with just such a cord, arm out in elaborate awkwardness to pin its high-wire crawl up and across the lofty ceiling. *Quality. Will derive. Peculiarity. Precisely.*

Then comes my first visit back to the doctor's, "a week out," as they say, from surgery. I'm shown the X-ray just taken, which turns out to be a comparative gesture, a wedding picture of both knees, side by side: my old "good" one—its bony parts still 100 percent human, doggedly holding up—and the fake, presumably better one. But the case-in-point, the replaced joint seems curiously not there at all, no detail on the shiny dark film clipped to the whiteboard. Between a top and bottom run of bone that appears to be my leg, my new knee is a pale squarish shape afloat. It's like a blindfold on a crime victim or some embarrassed porn star.

Oh yeah, I think, my metal and plastic bits *can't* speak to an X-ray, so nothing shows up in the picture. Right. But we talk as if we do see something. And hence its name so long ago from

Wilhelm Röntgen, the X-ray's nineteenth-century inventor dreaming a force that would, in fact, do the mathematical right thing and, yes, smartly "solve for x." Still, there's not much on the screen. Which is to say, the secret part tells all. As with any imaginative act, you fill in the blank and hope that the crucial elements are in place to straighten and bend, opening the way from here to there.

First sentences of a story move exactly out of that nothing and, especially in Flannery O'Connor, are often more fuse than trigger. I love first lines beyond all reason. Some "solve for x" straightaway, or begin to. "The grandmother didn't want to go to Florida," O'Connor wrote, igniting her greatest hit "A Good Man Is Hard to Find." It's the grandmother; first place in that sentence, queen-bee subject position, elevated and set apart, pinned to the page by the word *the*. And why not? Is she not our earpiece, our link to the terrible unknown to come, the brain that pretty much every sight and sound will be funneled through? "Didn't want to go"—say those words slowly. Their mostly single-stress exacts a stubborn breath between. *Didn't want to go*, their no no no no wrenching the story into a very bad mood already crabby enough for even the expert cranky among us to recoil into semi-amusement, however ominous it feels. Finally, "to Florida," O'Connor tells us. And about that, enough said: tacky land of the snowbirds, fountain of youth long hoodwinking smarter adventurers than those on this story's bad, bad road trip. This grandmother clearly has her own destination and delusions. The story will be—like many of this writer's—a battle of wills from the get-go.

So much of the narrative kicks in here, with such matter-of-fact fierceness. It's a treasure trove of first sentence: character, tone, suggestion of plot, the start to genuine drama. And a most credible voice, the hardest thing for a writer to winnow new against all the hot air available in life or in what others have already written. O'Connor made it a point to stay clear of Faulkner, for instance, as he "might swamp my small boat" though she welcomed the waters of more distant writers, Conrad and Hawthorne in particular. Her handling of this opening is an example of what she called her "one and a half" approach: two-thirds third person, one-third omniscience, a method she mostly but not always used. Via that third person, we get an inkling of the grandmother: she's no-nonsense and silly at once. (Third-person limited—or close—I've heard fiction writers call it, and what O'Connor must mean: this seeing everything from a single character's point of view, as a way a mind reader might know it.) That last, omniscient third of her equation (a third eye?) is most definitely godlike, if you can imagine a higher being this edgy, gearing up to "solve for x" with such riveting, toxic machinery in tow. Godlike. You hear that in the emphatically stressed cadence. This narrator knows her stuff. No reason, she just does. *The grandmother didn't want to go to Florida.* The sound itself convinces, especially that midsentence rise and rigid weight coming down hard on the word "want." But the not-quite-right, the contrary, and then some other thing desired and looming in the pauses: that's what propels us forward.

O'Connor has other first sentences to revere even as they jump up to bite us. Occasionally she makes it two sentences, as in "The Comforts of Home":

> Thomas withdrew to the side of the window and with his head between the wall and the curtain he looked down on the driveway where the car had stopped. His mother and the little slut were getting out of it.

Or in "A Circle of Fire," with the high drama watercolor rinse of landscape going strange, and then a question to seal that:

> Sometimes the last line of trees was a solid gray-blue wall a little darker than the sky but this afternoon it was almost black and behind it the sky was a livid glaring white. "You know that woman that had that baby in the iron lung?" Mrs. Pitchard said.

Or the beautifully rendered first sentence from "Revelation," one of the last stories she wrote. Built on a trick of reversals and repetitions and smart-ass dependent clauses, it inexplicitly sobers, coming down on the gravity of its final word.

> The doctor's waiting room, which was very small, was almost full when the Turpins entered and Mrs. Turpin, who was very large, made it look even smaller by her presence.

Elizabeth Bishop, in one of her letters to Robert Lowell, wisely observed that O'Connor could "cram a whole poem-idea into a sentence," all of the above examples included, I would guess, though the poet's list of such lines was probably endless, if such a count were even possible. A whole story idea, that too, no doubt, shrunk down to one edgy sentence. A turn and a counter-turn. A no. A yes. Then something more surprising. So maybe it isn't odd after all, O'Connor's way with the linoleum block, her approach to that medium a matter of working in reverse—not the first choice of most artists—by gouging out the main detail in her drawing on that thick surface, letting the background stand untouched and, once inked, do the real work. Which is to say, she left the blackened context to outline and nail down her central images that remain blistering white in her cartoons. The truth is she made a negative before the picture emerged. Really, she made an X-ray each time; it's the darker bits of the margin, in the side vision, that mean and mean business.

In O'Connor's stories, such roundabout method governs much more than the sentence. The following paragraph opens "A Temple of the Holy Ghost," front-loading it, as is often the case in her work, with enormous humor. (As a product of thirteen years of parochial schools, I can say—trust me—she's got the savage hilarity exactly right.) What's so intriguing is that her raised secondary figures appear first, two visiting cousins who set the stage and slowly reveal by the paragraph's end the real heart and sensibility of the story: a younger girl, her "sass" established, and now her "aloneness," through which very unsettling realizations will come. In some sense, the passage is a dry run for the shape of meaning in the whole piece.

All weekend the two girls were calling each other Temple One and Temple Two, shaking with laughter and getting so red and hot that they were positively ugly, particularly Joanne who had spots on her face anyway. They came in the brown convent uniforms they had to wear at Mount St. Scholastica but as soon as they opened their suitcases, they took off the uniforms and put on red skirts and loud blouses. They put on lipstick and their Sunday shoes and walked around in high heels all over the house, always passing the long mirror in the hall slowly to get a look at their legs. None of their ways were lost on the child. If only one of them had come, that one would have played with her, but since there were two of them, she was out of it and watched them suspiciously from a distance.

Distance again, which does appear crucial in so many ways for O'Connor; distance made close, belied by humor and by the most lippy energy of her narrative voice. As "A Temple of the Holy Ghost" goes on, the realm of dream, or more accurately dark and comic daydream, is where the main character, "the child," will embolden herself by imagining a heroic martyrdom. She's "in a pair of tights, in a great arena, lit by the early Christians hanging in cages of fire, making a dusty light that fell on her and the lions." And finally a more disturbing reverie takes over the child, such ironic distance in the narrative voice dropping as everything moves from puzzle to a wordless wonder, where what she's heard from her cousins after their night at the county fair comes back to haunt.

Their story is of the so-called "freak" seen in a sideshow, lifting "its" dress to show a shocking physical secret underneath, first to the men's side of the tent, then to the women's, this "freak" who holds forth: "God made me thisaway and if you laugh He may strike you the same way. This is the way He wanted me to be and I ain't disputing." Then the loud silence of both crowds in response. Or so the child, half-awake but lost in the riddle of that silence, dreamily and uncomfortably keeps picturing on the long car ride that ends this story. Because the girl can't figure it out, it's a vision of sorts that this writer gives us.

One of Flannery O'Connor's cartoons for her college newspaper, *The Colonnade*, shows three young women. Two stroll and talk, one of them casting a wary eye on the third figure, lower right, done up in the fashionable plaid skirt and striped socks of the period, this one a young woman, too, but drawn upside-down though apparently also walking, her long legs scissoring forward and back, as she holds up a book to read. Given the date, 20 March 1943, and the caption—"Coming Back Affects Some People More Than Others"—it's probably just after spring or Easter break. The girl-in-reverse hides behind her book and is defiant, her frown about equal to what appears on the tallest upright figure who's stolidly normal, headed in an opposite direction. They face each other, or could, about to pass and go on. I can see it was hard work, tending to the detail on the linoleum block, mouths to curve down and not up. One tiny false move with the cutting tool could make a disastrous smile. There's enough stubborn cheer, after all, in the nonchalant daring of the young woman who seems fine, flipped head to the ground, doing what she's meant to do. Which is to read and read, going elsewhere, upside down if she has to be. And not to care a dollop what anyone thinks. It doesn't take much to understand this image as partly self-scrutiny, a self-portrait—a thing all art reveals on some level—the self in question here both serious and amused. This might be, in theory at least, a picture O'Connor would have preferred over the photograph that ended up on the back jacket of *Wise Blood*, which, she complained to her friends Robert and Sally Fitzgerald, made her "look like a refugee from deep thought."

Humor in cartoons—any book on the subject says this more or less—means seizing, above all, something so commonplace that it's ignored. And busting that open somehow. For starters, people do walk to places all the time, though only a few of us read as we walk. According to Arnie Levin, whose drawings have appeared regularly for decades in *The New Yorker*, "a cartoon is basically a story. It's a moment . . . singled out as different from the next moment." And to manage that, one "must be able to recognize the patterns of life, the natural rhythms, the clichés, and when they're broken because the broken ones are the interesting ones." You have "to train your senses to react," he advises, "and catalogue little instances."

O'Connor's habit is to begin in clarity and end in mystery, one of the two opposing options of dramatic movement and shape we have as writers. I like this notion of "little instances" as a way to get there, this "training the senses" to absorb image, gesture, situations from a lived life, even a life over-lived unto cliché, for satire's sake—often O'Connor's preference initially—with its impulse to see the "broken" and what's familiar, too, hated or loved before it breaks. (The large woman of the very small doctor's office in "Revelation" was one such find, a happy by-product of the writer's own long hours waiting in just such a place: Mrs. Turpin was based on "one of those country women," O'Connor wrote to her friend Cecil Dawkins, "who just springs to life; you can't hold them down or shut their mouths.") Finally, it's the "react" in Levin's advice which is crucial. And that part can never be clichéd. However loosely sketched or close to caricature O'Connor's characters may seem at first, sooner or later their more startling complexities come to light. It takes time, and considerable patience. A writer reacts, then, by way of the story, the poem. That's the triumph. "The whole story is the meaning," O'Connor once wrote in obvious relish answering a critic who irritated her no end.

An early piece of Elizabeth Bishop's that O'Connor probably saw (and thus perhaps part reason behind her telling the poet, "I have great respect for your work") was "A Summer Dream," set in a most sorry place with a "sagging wharf" where "few ships could come," its opening two lines already putting the fabulous promise of its title out of the question. The narrative continues, clearly enough, to draw in a "gentle storekeeper / asleep behind his counter" and a "kind landlady." In addition, we're told of "two giants, an idiot, a dwarf," this last a dressmaker, a "shrunken seamstress" who smiles. More, the idiot "could be beguiled / by picking blackberries" and one of the giants—son of the landlady—has a "stammer" and can be found "grumbling on the stairs / over an old grammar." Thumbnail sketches, darkly whimsical, caught and held briefly by the abrupt pause of each line break, her spare imagery a kind of sharp, softening tribute to aid and abet this place that seems curiously interior, where

> By the sea, lying
> blue as a mackerel
> our boarding house was streaked
> as though it had been crying.

Bishop's animated, personal style of drawing has a ghost life here; you can almost sense a wonky extension cord lurking somewhere. This worn-out place *comes to* under that influence, the room's "geraniums / crowded the front windows," its floors a crazy secondhand patchwork that "glittered with / assorted linoleums." Later, there's an owl to hear at night and a lamp whose flame was such that "the wallpaper glistened," a more secret world shared with an intimate someone. And in the redeeming contrast that ends the poem—the giant son as "morose" as his landlady mother is "cheerful"—the whole thing slips into high lyric and what we might call a love poem: the bedroom "cold," the "feather bed close," the third-person "we" hearing more things in the dark to create a kind of cleaving in these opposing forces. Bishop makes us see that. Asked once in an interview if she had revised down for these details, whether "A Summer Dream" was drawn from "something larger" she had written about a "dying seaside town," the poet said no, though in fact it had come out of a trip to such a place in Cape Breton. She hoped to convey "some idea of what the people there were like."

But face it: the poem's description of those people, in part made visible by what now might be called politically incorrect language—the giant, the idiot, the dwarf—could be straight out of a story by O'Connor, though she would have worked the comic edge much harder and siphoned it through a character with more damning if less visible disabilities.

I can prove that. I can make up O'Connor's version this instant, the very first paragraph she might have managed from such detail. I can be a living, breathing Ouija board, O'Connor writing right through me, and I can only hope her lost spirit is forgiving, and Bishop's too, for that matter. Here goes—

When Mrs. Manorhouse arrived from the wharf to claim her room reserved months ago, she saw the dwarf first, done up in a perfectly awful smock way too big for her, her feet propped on a chair, sewing in the parlor just like an ordinary person. Oh dear, poor little, little thing, Mrs. Manorhouse thought, what kind of place is this? She pictured that funny museum back in Schnoorerville, its dioramas not exactly dollhouse size, but the scale definitely down, a first step to disappearing. And here she was, having kept her figure after all these years—well, barely—but she did wonder next how wide the beds might be in this place, or if she'd be eating off tiny plates too, the spoons just a wispy suggestion of a spoon like those in Aunt Virginia's old demitasse set at home, the one Winston almost threw out in a rage before she had said, "Don't you dare touch those, Buster!" and distracted him with a very nice lunch. She tried to smile but that little dwarf person ignored her completely, and kept on pushing her shiny needle in.

If I've caught O'Connor even remotely here—though a bit too cartoonish, I'm afraid—Mrs. Manorhouse is in for it, big time. She's sunk herself already, and this beginning is a narrowing of human empathy that will continue, enlarge in irony, and probably suffocate in the end.

O'Connor's genius comes down to this if you read enough of her: one element askew, at odds, and she's off. That cartoonist is right about noticing the broken thing. For O'Connor, this approach must be part of her "habit of art," a phrase she loved from Jacques Maritain and returned to many times in her letters and essays. You look close for some quirk—or it suddenly finds you—but through the distances involved, what is seen and heard turns to a telling. Her ear is wicked enough to be really good, and so tempting, her grip on us that strong. All it takes for me is, say, the thought of my husband talking years ago about the threat of childhood disease, his own brush with death as an infant, the crucial medical intervention, and our neighbor hearing his story, leaning forward, blurting out: "That's nothing! Without my doctor back then, I'd be cross-eyed!" But there's more: our neighbor *was* cross-eyed. Oh my god, I think, I do have a life. And it's straight out of Flannery O'Connor.

So many "little instances" in her real stories first subtract and judge through humor, then multiply into something earnest, more solitary and slippery, often visionary. And even metaphor, its like-unto-like, does this as a sort of miniature, a thing familiar made strange, too, but this time by some wild yet credible comparison, a move O'Connor made with dark comic verve: the relatively healthy young man in her story "The Enduring Chill," for instance, who is so overwrought and disdainful, so sure of his imminent demise, that he "looked like one of those dying children who must have Christmas early."

As for this knee business, my own familiar-turned-strange, week follows week and it continues to ache, is swollen to what feels like concrete that I'm peg-legging around, still scaring the cat. More often I'm lying down in this recovery, off the narcotics now, which made me sick; what a disappointing addict I've turned out to be! But I'm really cranky, complaining to endlessly good-hearted Bill Clausen, my physical therapist: What's really normal, Bill? What's normal pain and what isn't? I'm thinking maybe they put my knee replacement gizmo in backward or upside down or it's just the wrong damn size. I'm to bend and bend, the knee exercises excruciating, the stitches still red and scabby, and I can see the scar's Frankenstein line isn't changing much. These things I do to earn a decent range of motion, tight and tighter; won't they rip the wound apart? And no, says Bill. There are layers, and deeper layers. It heals underneath first, he tells me, and most strongly there.

He shrugs. He's amused by my disbelief. But I'm trying to believe, flashing on the veritable microscopic parfait that must be my knee inside: all these overlays, some merged already, some closer to the surface still madly knitting away to connect, burning calories as we talk to the end of his patience with me. "There's a certain grain of stupidity that the writer of fiction can hardly do without," O'Connor wrote, "and this is the quality of having to stare, of not getting the point at once." At home, adrift on the bed all afternoon, I think about those deeper lines of tissue, their reach and overreach making their case to the twin gods of healing and giving up.

Okay. Deeper lines and reach and layers. There were gifts between Bishop and O'Connor; the poet especially seems to have sent many things over the years—books and photographs and such vivid descriptions of Brazil, once zeroing in on her visit to the island of Marajo where "huge herds of . . . very friendly and lazy buffalos . . . come and lean on the houses (knocking) them flat." O'Connor replied that "the pictures are wonderful, and I am glad to know you got back from looking at the Amazon and were not leaned upon by the tame buffalos and pushed over. I kept having that mental picture, sort of in snapshot form—'one of the rare photographs of the poet, Miss Bishop,' and the tame buffalo, smiling, leaning you down. My notion of the jungle is all out of Frank Buck."

Once Bishop mailed her something touched directly by a

homemade eccentricity they both loved. In a letter to Lowell, the poet claimed it was "acquired at a vegetable stand—a crucifix in a bottle" that she'd sent O'Connor from Brazil, "all the accoutrements, gilded, and a rooster, nails, etc.—and I offered it to her. She said she'd like it—she'd been trying to write a story for a long time about a man who had the head of Christ tattooed on his back—she saw him in the paper." Rereading that letter, I imagine a pause here, a couple of seconds at least, and then: "I think we have a lot in common," the poet told Lowell. And to O'Connor: "I am wondering if by any chance you might sometime like to take a trip to South America to visit me?" Then she detailed the way such an adventure would go.

In O'Connor's return note to thank Bishop, she wrote that she'd been struck particularly by that rooster. "Did you observe that the rooster has an eyebrow . . . I am altogether taken with it. It is what I am born to appreciate." Given the increasing threat of her lupus, she added a more poignant thought, for all its nonchalance: "If I were mobile and limber and rich I would come to Brazil at once after one look at this bottle."

Hyperbole, yes, but entirely gracious and funny and true enough, the "one look" it would take "if I were," wrote O'Connor. Of course, sure, all those impossible things. Such a remark is in keeping with the playful, smart, affectionate tone of O'Connor's other letters to Bishop. Though she seems conscious of writing to a writer, it's the friendship that's clear, and certainly O'Connor is answering in kind. Yet Bishop was a semipublic ally, too, working repeatedly with their mutual friend, Robert Lowell, to nominate her for various literary prizes. And in Bishop's first note to Lowell about *The Violent Bear It Away*, she enthusiastically embraced the book. Parts of it, particularly "that first section," seemed to her "superb" and "like a poem. In fact, she's a great loss to the art, don't you think?" Clearly, this time, Lowell did *not* think, but Bishop eased tactfully to O'Connor's defense when she responded to his letter. "Yes, the Flannery book is a bit disappointing, I'm afraid," she wrote—"one wishes she could get away from religious fanatics for a while. But just the writing is so damn good compared to almost anything else one reads—economical, clear, horrifying, real."

Again, what's normal pain, and what isn't? It heals first, nearer to the bone. And little instances beget bigger. These two writers were matter and antimatter, each beholden to the other, Bishop in her exotic places, working to make all the lush details close, somehow familiar in her poems, while O'Connor, kept confined by illness and perhaps temperament, stays home to find the strangest characters and secret lives there. But they did have a lot in common, as Bishop pointed out to Lowell. And the main medium of their personal exchange was a perfect choice—arm's length and at a distance—given how naturally reserved each writer seemed to be: those letters between them—like drawing, like writing stories or poems—a shared discipline of rich, solitary attention.

The truth is I'd really like to see that rooster myself. Even more, I like the idea of both women, in different parts of the hemisphere, eye to eye with it at some point, the same creature and its one weird brow, each writer trying to figure how in the world it even got in that bottle.

Other makings, other transformations, amaze no less. About linoleum block printing, I recently found this startling claim: you can make your own tools, it's simple enough. A book from my public library promises as much. You buy the wooden handles, but the curious part is that any old umbrella will do for the knife edge. Its steel ribs—or stretchers, they're sometimes called—are cut with needle-nose pliers, and you grind the tip and then slip the new homemade blade into that store-bought handle and tighten—assuming your umbrella, semi-trashed by rain and wind and hail, is ready for dissection.

There's a time-travel element here, a moment right out of the Iron Age: from scratch, your own tools. I wonder if O'Connor ever got wind of this trick, so sensible and magical, a lowlife alchemy. Junk becomes a thing to make a thing. It might trigger the possible, beautiful or not quite, and at least the never-imagined-before, whether you proceed as most artists do with that linoleum block or in the reverse way, as O'Connor did, gouging on target to cut the main image, the heart of her design, to nothing, allowing what remains to orbit at the edges and define it all. Umbrella rib turned blade. That is a transformation, of sorts, though fairly modest, not nearly the alteration O'Connor wanted in her stories, her "moment of grace" a much harder change to pinpoint. After all, a story, she wrote, was "good" only to the extent that it "successfully resists paraphrase" and "hangs on and expands in the mind." Careful, that sharp edge—as tool or tone—to cut but not to wound. And be memorable.

O'Connor's grace—and here I'm guilty of paraphrasing the writer—has to be quick, to surprise us out of ourselves the second it surprises and distances her characters from their own damaged lives. Meaning it had to leap out at her, too, completely unexpected, as if the story made itself. This echoes Robert Frost's famous mantra—his "no surprise for the writer, no surprise for the reader"—and O'Connor herself predicted that fiction was moving more and more "toward poetry." This from a prose writer whose love for image was as immediate and as surrounded by silence as a poet's, the very best of our lot. And Bishop would most certainly agree, in her case at least, repeating to her what she wrote to Robert Lowell in a letter to O'Connor: "Of course, I also feel you're probably a great loss to poetry."

Those "experiences of mystery" as she called them, do "hang on and expand in the mind" and, quite literally, take us out of ordinary narrative time via rage or despair or plain puzzled wonder. Out of dire loss, her characters honest-to-god see things, sometimes in a thirteenth-century visionary way, a time and a mindset O'Connor only half joked she really lived (versus Thomas Merton's more up-to-date fourteenth century). This might be a matter of her astonishing way with "horror, delicacy, accuracy, and no fuss," Bishop told her in a letter in 1960, unlike their "contemporaries" who suffered from sounding "gabby and over-earnest, or precious."

In "Revelation," her more and more appalling Mrs. Turpin—that woman too large for the doctor's waiting room—is witness to one bizarre, democratic expanse by the story's end: "a vast horde of souls" entering heaven, a makeshift company of "white trash . . . black niggers in white robes." All this she sees, plus "battalions of freaks and lunatics shouting and clapping and leaping like frogs" and only at the very end of the procession, as if in disappointing afterthought, "a tribe of people" like herself and her husband "who always had a little of everything, and the God-given wit to use it right."

Or there's quieter compulsion and release, as in O'Connor's favorite story, "The Artificial Nigger," where the most embarrassing Mr. Head, crushed nearly senseless with guilt by his public denial of his grandson, goes from hopeless to ravaged to "what time would be without seasons and what heat would be without light," finally understanding what mercy might be, if he were so lucky. And that grandmother again, the grandmother who didn't want to go to Florida, marks her experience of genuine grace by a simple gesture, her hand out briefly to the murderer, the Misfit. "Her head clears for an instant," O'Connor tells us in an essay, paraphrasing in spite of herself the idea that the grandmother "realizes, even in her limited way, that she is . . . joined to him by ties of kinship which have their roots deep in the mystery she had been merely prattling about so far." This writer leads her characters into a kind of eternal zone beyond human measurement where the edges that force their radiant moment are abruptly blackened, inked away to mere backdrop. Caroline Gordon in a blurb for *The Violent Bear it Away* compared her to William Blake, a claim Bishop tried to unpack in a letter to O'Connor—"Perhaps she means . . . the same sense of grief and surprise."

That Elizabeth Bishop mimes in a late poem called "Poem" a grace equally complex by way of loss and sudden gesture might have pleased O'Connor. Here the poet slips through her own keyhole of time partly by "switching tenses," she said in an interview once, giving "the effect of depth, space, foreground, background." In that piece, though, past and present merge through a central image, a painting she remembers as one her great uncle did of a place where she too once lived, taking her back there, its cows "two brushstrokes each," the "wild iris, white and yellow / fresh-squiggled from the tube." And—"Heavens, I recognize the place"—it all comes alive, then disappears in a single long look. The thing "done in an hour, 'in one breath,'" but "life and the memory of it so compressed / they've turned into each other." More, and more sadly—"our earthly trust," and "Not much," she decides:

> About the size of our abidance
> along with theirs: the munching cows,

the iris, crisp and shivering, the water
still standing from spring freshets,
the yet-to-be-dismantled elms, the geese.

Future and past, visionary and right here. Near such a tree on
the Purdue campus—not an elm, really a sweet gum whose small
spiked husks hang in fall like the most grisly eighth-century
weapon—I'm talking to Adam Lefton, a fiction writer. And be-
cause this place I teach has graduated so many astronauts, this
tree was a gift. Once a sapling sprouted in outer space and given
to the campus some years ago by a grateful former student after
his many turns around the Earth and back, it invites down whole
flocks of gorgeous bandit-looking cedar waxwings in spring.
And it is spring, or almost. I'm nearly two months out from
my surgery, and this space tree, this interplanetary sweet gum
makes an Eden for smokers, one of the few places left at school
that welcomes them. Adam could be the first man or the last,
and he's smoking, though shortly he will quit for good. I've just
parked my car here and struggled only a little to stand upright
and walk these few steps.

He tells me my new fake silvery knee that I can only imagine
in there, buried inside my thumping about with a cane, means
this and this alone: when the robots do come, they will recognize
me as one of their own. He blows a lungful of smoke thought-
fully, pointedly away from me.

And here's the deal, Adam says. I mean, the rest of us will be
shuttled into pens or lowered into holes. But you—because of
your knee, your knee!—you'll be up there with the robots and
you'll look down and notice us. Then you'll turn to the robots
and you'll tell them: Hey, I know those people. They're okay. Let
them out!

I have to say, life has its moments of grace, too. First O'Connor,
then Bishop, have prepared me.

Charm

Soon we will all be returning to
Emily Dickinson's dark closet.
—Charles Simic

It's dangerous.

Years ago I went with my son Will, a high school cellist, to check out various music schools. We found ourselves in a famous teacher's studio, invited in to observe a lesson. A young player was running through one of the cello's beloved standards, Tchaikovsky's "Rococo Variations," a wandering fierce torment lifted skyward, pure semiconsciousness brought to dear life. That kid sounded good, maybe great. How could I know? I sat there pretty much transfixed.

The piece wasn't long, at least it didn't seem very long, and came to an end perfectly triumphant. There was a long pause. Either the room got larger or smaller, I couldn't tell.

Nice, said the famous teacher finally, very nice. I see you've worked hard. You cut the notes, you had energy, stayed with it. Do you know what was missing?

What? whispered the poor boy. Will and I could barely hear him.

Charm, said the famous cellist, leaning forward and smiling

Charm? And I thought: what a blow. Devastating! I mean, how do you learn *that?* You might need a head transplant, a whole character, take-on-reality-your-entire-life transplant. . . .

Okay, charm means irresistible, surprising, often read as *good for you*, designed to win over, a sweet nature shrewdly projecting confidence and concern, engineered to put the world and self at ease. So many books claim to teach this sort of charm, of course the veneer of manners and etiquette but behind that, a view governed by the often sensible, like what I found in *The Woman You Want to Be: Margery Wilson's Complete Book of Charm* from the early 1940s (and registered, by the way, with the Library of Congress the same year as works by E. B. White, Eudora Welty, Margaret Wise Brown, Wilhelm Reich, an unlikely crew for the neighborhood bomb shelter). Here are two gems from Wilson's "how-to" regarding charm. First, more practical and specific: "Whenever a conversation seems to grow dull, throw in . . . contrast . . . which acts like yeast in dough. . . . Often this brings on a laugh . . . and will gain (you) the reputation of a wit." And second: "You must have at least two interests which apparently take your mind altogether off yourself. One must be *other people.*"

Whatever "apparently" means here, some individuals are naturals at this sort of charm because they are amused by most things and truly not self-absorbed, my old beloved cousin Elinor once among them. Years ago at our place for supper and veering toward blotto on gin, she stared into a family reunion picture of the Taylors (our shared maternal line), circa 1932, zeroing in on her cousin, who leaned forward among the others in some picnic grove, a relaxed, angular, edgy-handsome young man exactly her age. She—Elinor—sat demurely in the grass, one row down, equally stunning in her willowy dress.

Oh god, she blurted out at our table those sixty years later, there's Paul. He was *so* gorgeous, she said, laughing now. Why, I necked the pants off him!

She did NOT!—my mother, way younger, and the cousin-afterthought, later on the phone. (For the record and apropos of nothing, in the picture my mother, about twelve, looks exactly like Mick Jagger, though not so sullen.)

Perhaps because Elinor's remark was so outrageously unexpected, I am still charmed, happily smitten; clearly my mother was not. Which may lead to why charm packs its punch. Oh, it is dark! We both picked up on that.

Should it surprise that charm's real history begins way down the rabbit hole, and can be so dire? To charm someone long meant you scheme to be persuasive, sweetly or not, so you can scare to death or plot to death, to revenge or at least trick somehow.

This is the ancestral version of charm, an attempt to control fate by inventive, usually nefarious ways: pins in voodoo dolls, girls swooning at witchcraft trials, the way politicians running for office distort *the way it is* to influence the vote. *To charm*, the noun turned verb. This bad-for-you kind once came with instructions. As in (third edition, 1929) *Malay Poisons and Charm Cures*, which I found in a pharmacy library, a well-used crumbling book with irresistible, gruesome chapters like "Black Art in Malay Medicine," like "Spells and Soothsaying." But to be fair, there's "Charms and Amulets" not so much to attack but outfox any forest demons or block counterspells, for use in even clear-cut medical emergencies like snakebite and small pox. The book advises bile, blood, "prenatal language," worms, and "land bugs" for serious vigilance because it is wildly easy to be thrown off course in this life, straight into genuine dark.

Worldwide, such anxiety has seeded a lot of poems. Even John Keats fell for this, basing his long mostly ignored poem "Lamia" on an exquisitely striking woman cast as a snake poised to charm unwary men into deep trouble. In a more general way, it's simply fear lurking behind most situations perhaps. Press a bit and that fear could vanish. The world is hard but might click into easy. It *is* dodgy. You can't predict a memorable anything. Thus the lyric double-take explosive in a lot of poems.

Which is charm. There's no learning it because its fear and its pleasure *must* take by surprise. And if a breakneck not-quite harmony comes of all this, you never quite forget that jumpy thing still in your side vision, slight afterimage of panic.

Back to that mid–twentieth century charm book meant to instruct and smooth edges, I found this gem of warning: charm means the letter C foisted on *harm* as in beware, look out, there's danger you need to see. That crucial baseline dark could be the most irresistible thing about charm. Because *press*, then *release*—wow, you survived!

In poetry too there's a *come hither*, a *just wait*. Charm's double whammy is a fuse.

In fact, the shape of charm could be the shape of poetry as it arrives in our heads and moves down the page. (A) *say what?* (B) *Okay, okay, it's just that* . . . (C) *what?* That three-part structure makes other acrobatic stunts orderly and eternal: morning, noon, and night forever taking turns in the sky, or the classic "three acts" screenwriters love. The sound of questions, of exploration and assertion, of knowing nothing then pausing into *what next?* Push me, pull me and between that, the *hold this* of poems *while I fiddle over here for a while or a minute.* Ignore that man behind the curtain!—which itself equals charm. And then that thing you didn't know you already knew, there, from the start.

Such recognition can begin with a notable absence. In "A Partial Explanation," an early poem by Charles Simic, the speaker sits alone in a "grimy little luncheonette." And: "Seems like a long time / Since the waiter took my order." The delay stretches on, made visible by careful details in this poem's Act One: snow keeps falling darker out there, no one on the street. The parameters of room and world, the scene emptied out, the lineation paced evenly to suggest patience. Or boredom, the kind aimed at one uninspiring hungry minute onto minute made of orderly progression and elegant deadpan until, act two:

> A glass of ice water
> Keeps me company
> At this table I chose myself
> Upon entering.

The build to a simple glass of water is painterly really, that business of snow and dim, the waiter vanished to whatever dark underbelly, only the sound of the kitchen door "behind my back," which swallows him. Simic's repetitions release into real time, the words themselves, "seems" and "since," both suggesting duration even as we stay in that moment's pause. But the poem is comic; *best-friending* a glass of water? Pretty close to pathetic in that lonely room, mock-desperate. That most ubiquitous word in our language starts the final stanza—the last act—in a kind of great sigh to the interior life we're forever seeking in poems. "And" writes Simic, with meticulous wry delicacy,

> a longing,
> Incredible longing
> To eavesdrop

On the conversation
Of cooks.

What amusement here! The kitchen staff somewhere close, deep in gossip toward which the speaker leans. Irresistible, this unexpected closure. As poet James Tate wrote in an essay: "Each line written is searching for the next line." And Simic's staccato lines do seem to *enact* longing, the movement in a poem such a physical thing. And playful here, amid such gloom. Were I to run this poem through a charm-o-meter, that machine would start humming right up. But the piece is pretty much complaint, a favorite subject, a big fat gripe of many parts. Will the waiter return? Will the speaker ever be fed and happy? Other poets might follow deeper the thorny ways we self-pitying sorts always get neglected.

So why does this *charm*? Because despair is persuasive; it's addictive, even the tongue-in-cheek variety. We're always ready to be talked onto, then off the ledge, to step into the shoes of whatever *despairee*. A dark glimpse is charm's hook and charm's magnet. Because only the secret life will last, the ache for that and its forbidden conversations behind a door. Oh eternal outsider!—that would be you and me too. A feigned melodrama makes large of the little, the feigned part veering it a little funny, thus bearable.

In reality, this poem never ends but charms us back from danger into an endearing hopeless hope. Simic's resistance *countercharms* to shift the lens and thus the issue, *not* to be served lunch, not to be particularly *not* lonely but—please—to overhear, to be curious about a small private part of the world in the long wait for anything. We're reminded how small we are, how large and interesting everything *not-us*. Such a relief really. The poem lands with the generosity of Frost's richly-worn refrain: *you come too.*

One can time-travel on that thought, to something more peculiar. Think *snakes*, both godlike and alarmingly strange. And hold that a moment.

I read this the other day: they first started *charming* those reptiles in India, earlier in Egypt, way back before Beowulf. Count the variety: the python and the viper, the common enough poisonous cobra. Long ago, the charmed notion that some first snake loved music and its deepest genes were altered forever, though it is a ruse of sorts, as some poems are. One difference: snake charming is a business in India, a performance but, like poetry, an art to it, maybe a healing too since the charmer traditionally double-duties as shaman. Imagine a whole spellbound side street in Mumbai hypnotized, watching that snake, toxic and for sure scary and big, ordinarily a silent streak of danger through the world's cacophony, now rising docile from a basket, stately and disciplined, following a human lead, bedazzled toward heaven. *Charmed.* We think. And then there's the charmer himself, that superpower conduit between worlds—human and reptilian—bringing back glorious beyond-human sounds and images to translate. What a job description! I think how this happens. I think *poet.* Then I think *loner.* Or: *under the right circumstances time does stop like this,* the snake angling up to the piper who's armed with his flute-like gourd, his *pungi,* its melody ribboning out bent, then straightening. Each side charms the other right now. Which is to say *all the way back to the ancients.* Which means even in poems many listen *with* us: ghosts, the no-longers, and those yet to be.

Laura Jensen is a poet whose three books were much revered in the '80s. Their mysterious clarity, their remote feel comes through her braiding of opposite forces: dream and hard moments lived, image and statement, movement and stillness under the radar and quite fragile by way of what Norman Dubie has called in her work "that blinking that precedes great lyric recognitions." And not charming in the way humor can delight and sober you up for the long drive home, though her mulling and trance, like Simic's, seems triggered by hesitation and profound isolation. Still, she's the charmer charming the snake idle then urgent, refigured enough to charm *back* from—and to—a place much darker.

The poem "Calling" from Jensen's third book *Shelter* goes about its business quietly trip-wired in present tense, the "eternal present" I've come to call it, something timeless nabbed in sleep, slipping into language. "This world calls like a mother /

to come downstairs from your dreaming," the poet begins. "She
sets you to some task"—

> But it rains.
> And the world never stopped the rain
> for a minute.
>
> Did she ever set you hanging
> the laundry on the line
> from the corner of the house
> to the mast in the blackberries
> and have the rain make you
> take it all back, white sheet
> by white sheet, and blouse by blouse?
>
> Come down, come down and stop your dreaming.
> The house grew old as I grew old
> and has turned into a waiting.
>
> I have gone back time after time
> and I have gone back crying. He says
> I am like laundry at her door.
> A suitcase full of troubles.
>
> We do it at the laundromat.
> And I live in a sea of tears.

First, a statement presents the world and its demands. Then
a catch: "But it rains." Then a long winding question via flash-
backed ordinary details of blouse and sheet that trigger and
echo toward a near afterlife directive: "come down, come down."
Time passes into *old*—house and self—and so brilliant, that next
move into "a waiting." Deliverance, such as it is, comes by way
of metaphorical impulse which is, let's face it, a way to protect,
at least to distance the grief-struck unspeakable. This speaker is
"like laundry at her door," and by extension and straight meta-
phor "a suitcase full of troubles." And then the inclusive "we
do it," the commonplace laundromat evoked, sly-quickening an
analogy to release the speaker to *live in* and not merely be the
source of "a sea of tears." This final phrase is rescued from cliché

by a despair so large and beyond poetic fashion that it undoes for good.

And it *charms*, however troubling. That's partly the rhythm. To repeat and repeat, to go back to similar image and syntax. We might be struck dumb as that snake by now, or as burdened as this speaker who, nonetheless and against Norman Dubie's certainty, seems not blinking at all but eyes open, running through syntactical structures we love: the question, the out of nowhere imperative, the fragment, the near drumbeat simple sentence. She even couplets-up that final stanza where the *we*—she really does *royal we* it—is handed back to the smallest first person, that "I" awash in great waters.

That sea, by the way, is enormous. Tears: most private leakage on the planet, all cast here in a repetitive cadence, close to chant. In that structural repeat, we're down to a click, a whisper. The last turns are rigidly controlled through the most straightforward declaratives, plain old subject and verb: I have gone, she says, I am, we do. . . . Until that *sea of tears* overwhelms.

The secret about the charmed snake is this: it is terrified. Subtle proscribed moves in this timeworn practice only pretend ease and grace. Because the charmer, as he twists and pivots, raising, lowering his instrument, is read by the snake as *enemy* and *beware: an attack*. The snake, not a standard partner in crime but watching, rising up, rearing back, matching each sway and return of the charmer, wary, to protect, to save, *about to*. . . . The snake is poison, the charmer a trickster. Who's controlling whom? The poet writes, rewrites what the poem insists it dreams and the residue is left on the page, a trace, that snakeskin wrinkled, luminous, abandoned: *someone was here, is still here. This is how someone saw and felt and thought.*

Step back. That music? Pointless, and not what we thought at all. Snakes are deaf.

More about reversals, toothed charm enablers. Say you are writing some line you totally believe; it's huge, and it's about grief or time or beauty, each idea weighing about a thousand pounds and requiring a crane, a forklift, a nine-ton freighter to inch-eke forward over the ocean where even a whale thinks itself small.

But what if you turned what's big into the shockingly simple?

Imagine you flipped whatever large, stony-immovable thought, suddenly unearthing a thing so personal and surprising you scare yourself? "I hate them. / I hate them as I hate sex," Louise Gluck blurts out in her poem "Mock Orange" that seemed at first to be about those flowers, a line Tony Hoagland once said in a lecture "thrilled the whole world—such a radical but humanly comprehensible thing to say." For his part, James Tate as a very young poet took up, then altered another standard, how we love to love love. His "Coda" is an early poem. "Love isn't worth so much," he begins. So it's that easy, to throw such a good granny favorite—love itself—under the bus? Granny's secret name for anything is *what you thought you knew inside out.* But guess what? Granny's deluded. You don't.

The physicist Niels Bohr, discoverer of the electron and radioactivity, has said that the nature of a great truth is that its opposite is also a great truth. A door opens to a jarring uncertainty that's true true true regardless. *Entrance* suggests walkway, a plain enough noun, a passage, a time-soaked place. But as verb, it's scary as hell. You step out of time, shifting the stress to the first syllable of that word. To charm is to *en-trance.*

There's this. To be entranced means opposite things link sudden, surprising, *never what you expect.* To rivet. To loosen. To free things up. When I was an MFA student at the University of Massachusetts a hundred years ago, my teacher was the same James Tate who had recently written the line I just quoted. In workshop he was generous and funny and smart, attentive to our poems in roundabout ways. But my dream one night nailed it exactly—and has become a story I can't help telling again and again.

And maybe because it came to me mindless, in sleep. We were in workshop, all around the table as usual, and Tate—I swear it—kept throwing babies in the air, human babies in diapers and no hair. It was his laughter that got us, his wild delight as those infants took to flying above us, circling, and *they* giggled madly. The dream continued. Soon we were crazy-losing it too. Hilarious, "completely bonkers," I think, is the clinical term. I woke to a great pleasure. Was it happiness, this close to danger? I still remember that. Surely I was charmed: maybe we are always aloft, dreaming and rollicking. Back in the conscious world that morning, I . . . Yes, this is accurate, I thought, our class is *like* this. And now, years later? It's simply how poems work. Dream or not, something about metaphor startles, thus charms; it's a contact high, two unlike things inexplicably *liking* each other. However tragic Jensen's meditation, her governing impulse is metaphorical, thus an intricate ageless machinery transforms and widens. The world calls "like a mother," it's *like* taking down that "blouse by blouse" in the rain. One can arrive as "a suitcase full of troubles" at someone's front door; the mystery of that image opens then closes. And don't we all "live in a sea of tears"? The poet lifts this worn adage until it is edged and horrific and can crush us again, just like that.

Mysterious—what's memorable, what isn't. Surely charm is involved; one gets *charmed* by certain poems. As in: I know a few by heart without even trying. Like another early poem by James Tate, "Flight," which *reverts* to charm quite differently than Jensen's poem does, this one by great play "just as" the refrigerator starts singing, as "the fish are disgusted/and beat their heads blue/against a cold aquarium," as the speaker's two neighbors in the building "realize that they have not/made love to their wives since 1947." More: "the man downhall / is teaching his dog to fly." A veritable simulcast! And yes, a pointed absence turns out to be the main event, this poem an argument, a declaration: "Were you here." And so a serious reach for the beloved.

This piece from Tate's first book goes oddly and sweetly into a most ancient category: *love poem*, usually a sobering, urgent subgenre, the hardest to keep credible and unsentimental. Famously first setting the bar in English for the personal lyric *and* the love poem, some anonymous sort in the late 1400s began his brief "O Western Wind" aching for "small rain," and "Christ, that my love were in my arms, / And I in my bed again!"

This poignant scrap from the Middle Ages reminds us: one must be true to human experience. Which means both sorrow and the continuing wish for not-sorrow. We can hold off some of this. Metaphor rivets and loosens Tate's poem because its images get comic, sideways personified, each grounded to a darker surreal. His book *The Lost Pilot*—a Yale Younger winner—was published in 1967, so those husbands had been waiting to be amorous for twenty years. Dogs still have hope of flying in the poem; fish know their issues and act accordingly at great personal cost. Dust eventually not only *huddles*, it cooks up *conspiracies* the *we*— the poem's speaker and his beloved—"would not tolerate." And back to the offbeat prefiguring overture, the fridge sings like a cricket but a *glum* one needing a happy ending or serious comfort food. Metaphor's invention preanimates, predelights, and opens.

But always deep down in metaphor—as in charm—is a not-quite-equaling, an uneasy, knotty does-not-compute. Only opposing energies trigger "progression;" William Blake told us that long ago. We get off on reversals, things not exactly what they appear to be. In Tate's poem, quirky shifts of imagery and diction move down very short lines, tercet to tercet. That it all adds up to a "racket" that "multiplies" seems credible in the close quarters of an apartment building and via the poet's stepping back so clearly amused. Then there's the unwieldy matter of wonder, the large sidling up to the small, a perennial *this* against *that*. "Look, the world is everywhere: satellites, end tables, the pink and white poinsettias outside the church; reunions and degrees. All those radiant asterisks." says poet Terrance Hayes in his *Wind in a Box*, nailing the great weirdnesses around us and in us and linking us.

"Fancy, Come faster"—that was Gerard Manly Hopkins' parenthetical aside, the one Elizabeth Bishop relished in his long, earlier poem, the tedious, heavy-handed "Wreck of the Deutschland," about a real disaster at sea. His digressive note-to-self must have loosened his riveting, certainly for later poems, the luscious, head-over-heels charm-release of a line like "fresh-firecoal chestnut-falls; finches wings." A most astonishing music lay ahead of him. And the parenthetical itself, backhand and secret, would acquire superstar status in Bishop's poems to come.

Fancy as a noun isn't a word we love these days, and Hopkins did urgently exclaim but surely the whole business of poetry goes parenthetical at times, abruptly a small under-the-surface explosive. That's charm, any poem taking us on as accomplices. Finally, a place to hide and be welcomed! I'm forever quoting Auden, who said we don't hear but *overhear* a poem. It's inward, and only aimed peripherally at us. I need to add that one hears it musically, which is instant interiority. Poetry, after all, isn't a lawyerly tract, not a how-to about how to get the new dishwasher on wired alert.

My son on this point, years after that cello lesson and the teacher's seemingly cutthroat remark, my bringing it back with *Remember? That terrible thing he said?–*

It wasn't that bad, Will told me. I think I'd know exactly what to do. Look, the "Rococo Variations" is all about quick changes, up and down, wild sudden turns. If you deadweight it, you kill it. That kid was probably on every note like a brick.

He paused. In the bowing, in the notes, it's a matter of both hands, he said. Charm? That teacher was only saying, *pick up the pace, vary the tone, let it run through your fingers* . . .

But my son is a writer now, a teacher too. So it can't stop there.

Here's sure evidence of poetry's quick/slow double whammy of charm dark and light; this a piece written in 1935 by Irish poet Louis MacNeice.

SNOW

The room was suddenly rich and the great bay-window was
Spawning snow and pink roses against it
Soundlessly collateral and incompatible:
World is suddener than we fancy it.

World is crazier and more of it than we think,
Incorrigibly plural. I peel and portion
A tangerine and spit the pips and feel
The drunkenness of things being various.

And the fire flames with a bubbling sound for world
Is more spiteful and gay than one supposes—
On the tongue on the eyes on the ears in the palms of your
  hands—
There is more than glass between the snow and the huge
  roses.

When physicists kept at it in the last century to break down matter to the smallest bits imaginable, they sought a name for those almost-nothings. *Finnegan's Wake* records a triumphant cheer

("Three quarks for Muster Mark!") and one word got philtered in 1964 by codiscoverer Murray Gell-Mann. Apparently Joyce's choice of *quark* was a blurring, part cry of the gull, part last pub call, plus his turning the standard three *quarts* for a *Mister* Mark much odder. Of the six so-called "flavors" of quarks which include *Top, Bottom, Strange, Up,* and *Down,* the quark *Charm* is charming, I've heard, because of its lovely structural symmetry. All quarks have balance though, a built-in opposite particle, a conjoined twin, which means *Charm* has an *anticharm* lurking about, an antiquark of "equal magnitude but opposite sign."

Just so, there's a lot of quark and antiquark in MacNeice's poem; his noisy leaps and stops sound *incorrigibly plural* themselves, those on-again, off-again rhymes or how the graceful repetition of that intrepid word "and" (nine times!) helps this poem race and roil but keep its awe democratic, roughly equal, line by wild line. And the gorgeous varied syntax winds against that leveling to startle—"world is suddener" and "world is crazier"—two statements most seductive. Then that abrupt run of old Anglo-Saxon single stresses, a very ballsy "I pip the seeds and feel." Wow! And so on.

What charms me most though is the *anticharm* surprise of "spiteful" in there, an element edgy-imposed just when we're riding that wave of great release, all singing given over to cite the lush wonders of the world. (Oh that large welcome in the tangerine, bubbling flames flickering, the great presumed happiness "of things being various." Joy come to life! Clearly MacNeice had a good swig of the Kool-Aid Hopkins loved.)

On second thought, why be so surprised at this antiquark of "spiteful"? The shrewd "incorrigibly" and "crazier" is threaded in early, the poem's governing image of roses "spawned" in the first place to incite god knows "more than"—what?—his splendid flowers grown almost as strange as Plath's would be nearly two decades later, 1962, her poem the very unsettling "Tulips," its publication timed by season and weirdly but doggedly earmarked by *The New Yorker* for the spring issue nearest Easter, a day notoriously pink, afloat with such flowers (minus Plath's dark version, of course), morning of chocolate bunny-glad, and new shoes.

Meanwhile—*against,* says MacNeice, the great window's

glass. *Against*—key word and that "spiteful" to keep us—stop! *C-Harm*—in the middle of the vital push me/pull me moment, aware of possible human pain and its fireworks. Never an end to such looming.

So be it: charm = edge and threat = beauty a lot, or—more accurately—just barely.

Bring on the strange, the most dangerous, says charm as it stops and reverses any poem, pretending ease. Sure, not thinking a thing.

Diagnosis, Poetry,
and the Burden of Mystery

I look where no one dares,
And I stare where no one stares.
—John Keats

We come into this life with nothing, and fully decked out: fingers, toes. Plus the screaming. And the shorthand mission of poetry, if not everything else, is to think through that rich doubletake and dark. It's hard. Thus sooner or later "my mind's not right" may be what we all say. In Robert Lowell's poem "Skunk Hour," that sentence, "my mind's not right," is an honest-to-god last line in a stanza followed by silence visually rendered, the so-called "white space" on the page. A stanza break, that hold-your-fire to let the assertion hover.

This is Robert Lowell, his mind, more aptly his *speaker's* mind, in this piece dedicated to his friend Elizabeth Bishop from his 1959 groundbreaking book, *Life Studies*. The poem orbits profound troubles of self, here a pretty pathetic self, driving around at night in a village in Maine, up "the hill's skull" where "lovecars" have parked. (Would he be arrested these days, for such voyeurism? John Berryman, isn't there a law against this particular Henry?) "They lay together, hull to hull," he tells us—the cars themselves? teenagers breathless in those cars?—"where the graveyard shelves on the town." The ending sad ellipsis to that sentence, its dot dot dot, keeps his *not rightness* going. Because his mind isn't right, is it? He's just offered succinct proof. Another damning declarative rounds out the next stanza: "I myself am hell; nobody's here—" says Lowell, landing on a dash, Emily Dickinson's famous *no-more-words*. Yet Lowell being Lowell—not in a million years the secret forthright Dickinson—continues.

Certainly there are other ways to do this, call it quits. Think James Wright, who closes out one of his greatest hits with "I have wasted my life," an equally clarifying, exhausted gesture, but only after he's ticked off the lush particulars of early evening: a "bronze butterfly," a glorious distant view, "a leaf in green shadow." Note this: neither poet offers any practical solution. They're *just saying*, though perhaps those skunks of Lowell's raiding the trash in the moonlit night, how they "do not scare," suggests something more unsettling than simple hunger.

Nevertheless, here's a not-so-idle claim: poetry—perhaps all literature—is its best self when it takes no responsibility to fix a damn thing. Not poem-as-therapy despite the fact that, as Eleanor Wilner reminds me, Ezra Pound once insisted *cure* its highest aim, a major part of poetry's "cult of beauty." Still, it's not exactly a matter of pontificating for a better tomorrow. Suck it up, friends. The thing is you can notice trouble, even conclude, as in "my mind's not right," as in—you know what? I *have* wasted my life—and there's a barely discernible click inward, one of the great rewards of poetry. If there's an arc forward—prognosis, the possible *due course* of diagnosis—it's more like Cassandra forced to see the future destruction of Troy, unable to stop it. Which is to say, literature is no treatment as such. It's bringing patterns to life. Diagnosis. Look hard, and a curiously charmed, more tentative *shared* intelligence lets it all sink in.

For his part, Robert Lowell has reached rock bottom. And Wright's struck dumb in his hammock until summer with its cowbells and sunlight feels multiple and eternal and swallows him. We keep reading. Sometimes the page is a mirror, decent enough company however painful a pleasure, this tangled slough of life distilled to a few moments of meditation called a poem.

It can plenty unnerve, such looking. My own memorable case-in-point orbits the privilege given me to attend the Gross Human Anatomy course, the so-called "cadaver lab," generously allowed in by anatomist James Walker of the Indiana University Medical School at Purdue University, where I've taught in the English Department many years. That, and the chance to understand the body by way of pencil and paper in the life drawing class offered by artist Grace Benedict in Art and Design. This double amazement all due to a Faculty Fellowship to study something well outside my comfort zone. I hate that phrase "comfort zone." But you leave it. Then it leaves you blinking and stranded.

Here's a raging simplicity: what we write is seeded in real life. Duh. Consider the late nineteenth century and its Sherlock Holmes. Because under that crafted character once lived a person, a diagnostician who memorably astonished his students at the University of Edinburgh, including the popular writer Arthur Conan Doyle when he studied medicine there. Dr. Joseph Bell knew more than enough. He could spot some poor guy limping down Marchmont Road, proclaim the problem not hip or knee but a stroke, a "shock," *how* the fellow leaned sideways. "Never trust to general impression," Bell wrote, "concentrate upon details." So rattling around Conan Doyle's brain for years was this ultra-observant rock-star professor from medical school until *voila!*—the novelist lurking the whole time under *Dr.* Doyle finds Sherlock Holmes, crack detective who could put two and two together and get some shimmering five out of it. Of course farther back lies something more personal. A very early classmate of the writer himself remembered "that untidy boy with his strange power of observation."

The take-away? Go for surprising *and* inevitable. It's riveting, diagnosis itself. *This* plus *this* to some personal leap, a crucial poetic gesture. Imagine Conan Doyle's flashing in reverse *That's it! I'll bloody well make Joe Bell my sleuth!* Thus his old teacher remains adrift in medical history while the conjured-up detective keeps multiplying toward the future where he will save the day forever more, on large screen and small, our Sherlock more clear than the shadow maker himself. Conan Doyle, after all, loved to complain that his imagined protagonist got more letters than he did. And what about those earnest marriage proposals for his character, coming in the post?

Or there's the poet John Keats. His famous teacher in medical school, Astley Cooper, wrote sentences like: "Sorry indeed should I be to sport with the life of a fellow-creature who might repose a confidence either in my surgical knowledge or my humanity." Note: *my humanity*. Because Cooper had been a student of the revered John Hunter, whose museums in the UK are national treasures. Hunter, most brilliant teacher of all, raised that "surgical knowledge" to an art past science by collecting all that crawled or flew or once turned in a womb: newts and bees, crocodiles, frogs, human fetuses, owls. Anatomy as *comparative* anatomy was his focus, his humanity shrewd and welcoming; no, it's how we are so *like* one another! London's Hunterian Museum remains a vast shipwrecked ark, whole systems—digestive, circulatory, respiratory—pulled out from whatever creature. Displayed there, the whole merry, improbable crew of the planet in profound, unsettling equality.

I've heard this too, since childhood: *Blood tells*, meaning what your father did, your mother, way back behind them, your personal Adam and Eve, great great grand whoever back and so on, springing your family into its first misadventure. But it's your own take in that *telling*, where and what you've lived: Keats in the present tense of so much agony; a mother, a brother wiped out by TB, the horrors of early nineteenth-century medicine and city life, the very shape of that personal and public grief. If there's a bloodline back, it moves forward too, some of that morphing into poems for Keats, in tone if not particulars. And though a lot has been made of the flowers he doodled into his dissection notes, he was, in fact, a successful student. His decent marks prove that, not to mention the amused disbelief of his cohort that he did so well on exams *and* wrote poems. Further: the post of "dresser"—that is, dresser of wounds, a surgeon's assistant— was offered him early in his studies at London's Guy's Hospital, that cutting-edge Mayo Clinic wannabe of his era, a real distinction, being one of seventy or so awarded out of the some three hundred students enrolled. And later, after leaving medicine, he did decide to keep his notes and textbooks because "an extensive knowledge," he told his friend John Hamilton Reynolds, "it takes away the heat and fever; and helps, by widening speculation, to ease the Burden of the Mystery."

Curiosity—half wonder and strict attention, half distance— does live in his poetry, gotten largely perhaps from the grim discipline of staring deep into the ruined body in his daily rounds as dresser, his job to hold the patient down in surgery, vital in those days of no anesthesia and no antiseptics, fresh bandages required constantly. But first, diagnosis: *show me what's wrong, what hurts.* It's comparative and perhaps something seen and imagined. And wasn't that the habit of Keats' teacher too? Astley Cooper, as befits any student of John Hunter, like the continual left hand coming down relentless as in anything by Bach: *look hard, and how alike we are, alike, alike.* Careful. Be careful with your knife. So a huge part of surgical know-how not fiercely narrowed to *meticulous* goes straight to empathy and premonition. And for Keats, to an abrupt self-assessment after finding himself fatally close to nicking the wrong vessel. "My last operation," he told his friend Charles Armitage Brown, "was the opening of a man's temporal artery. I did it with the utmost nicety; but, reflecting on what passed through my mind at the time, my dexterity seemed a miracle, and I never took up the lancet again."

Images suggesting Keats' grueling days at Guy's Hospital—and the deathbed care of his brother Tom—did enter his "Ode to a Nightingale," the poet coming into heightened imaginative power. An entirely real nightingale is what he saw at his place in Hampstead the spring of 1819, his medical training complete but that life abandoned by then for poetry, his own tuberculosis no doubt coming clear to him as he set up that bird as a kind of straw bird, wrote to it and through it to world and self, his urgent wish to

> Fade far away, dissolve, and quite forget
> What thou among the leaves hast never known,
> The weariness, the fever, and the fret
> Here, where men sit and hear each other groan,
> Where palsy shakes a few, sad, last gray hairs,
> Where youth grows pale, and spectre-thin, and dies;
> Where but to think is to be full of sorrow . . .

The thing about medical diagnosis is, you start from scratch, almost. Doctors find a category first—what *class* of trouble?—and begin to narrow down partly via complaints of the patient, *symptoms*, the word from Greek, "that which befalls, a depar-

111

ture." Call them *images*: the groans, the trembling, the "spectre-thin" bodies that Keats must have seen. Technically these are called *signs* in diagnosis, what the physician observes or tests for now, as was done centuries ago. Hippocrates of the famous oath, say, who insisted that "spilling the waters"—urine—was a key element: cloudy or clear? blood in it? bubbles? All equals a bad liver. Or the ancient Egyptians, sure that if piss drew insects, boils would follow. And always its sweet smell helped to clarify things, and taste too, I'm told, diabetes, the word itself meaning "honey urine." Diagnosis, a slowly acquired art, deeply rooted in the senses and, with any luck, the imagination.

It's not automatic. A wise doctor goes semiblank in order to puzzle the wounded thing. The born-to pattern of the body; what's messed it up? Sherlock Holmes always takes a second look "when a fact appears to be opposed to a long train of deduction." A *does not compute* starts poems too. The mind *is* a cat—intent on that wily mouse under the table about to screw up the nice dinner party—plus context, remember John Hunter? So everyone gathers there, happily oblivious for the moment, forks raised, mid-bite.

Which is to say, don't you have to cherish that folly-rich human backdrop for dear life? Spitting up blood, aware full well he might never grow old, know love, write poems, think thoughts, didn't John Keats desperately want such things? Thus that poignant nightingale on and on, out in the yard.

Meanwhile my husband and I go to Edinburgh for six months. It's *lovely, brilliant,* most beloved adjectives in the UK. Back home, his eye on our cat and our house, Gary Stuart, a visiting geneticist at Purdue, is living at our place on Maple Street. He e-mails about a mysterious pooling in the basement. I'm reading his words five time zones away at the latitude of Moscow or Hudson Bay, in a flat (a flat!), three floors above Strathearn Place, the rain a lush, blurry sepia. Gary Stuart writes that

> clearly the water was dripping from above, from the down-stairs bathroom. Inspecting the next level, I found a one inch diameter pool of water . . . Now to check the top floor bathroom! Completely dry—and I was confused until I saw lime

built up on the hot water line. Sure enough, holding my fingers there produced wet fingers! My guess is that this minor leak has been in process for quite a while. . . .

So, I suspect the problem is at the hot water tap, the top floor sink. I suspect it's easy to fix (tighten a junction or replace a rubber fitting) and would be happy to give it a try, but I thought I would ask your permission first, since problems that look simple can sometimes become hard in old houses.

Certain phrases here reveal the messy underpinnings of a house, but how nuanced by voice. *I found* and *now to check* (that exuberant exclamation point!) and *I was confused* and *my guess is* and the modest *I merely* until it's *I suspect*—twice—a kind of ending couplet riff of intense thinking, the joy of the finding-out politely masked by that *easy to fix* and its specific *tighten a junction or replace a rubber fitting*, the generous *would be happy to give it a try*, the hesitant *ask your permission first* because of course, of course, the whole compelling problem with art or science might lie in the darkly prophetic phrase *problems that look simple can sometimes become hard.*

In Stuart's elegant thinking lies genuine narrative movement: detail, a path of exploration in a very small space: room and basin, story and poem, all at first glance rather unremarkable, finite spaces. It looms up into a kind of clairvoyant *eureka* moment you could call lyric. Or closer, the more interior *I suspect, I suspect* to be savored. You could call this scientific. Or common sense racing toward diagnosis, nearly song in the process. You could say, as novelist Janet Burroway has, that "only trouble is interesting." You could, one *could*, for poems too. Back to a more workaday realm, such relief and good fortune for us far from home, our house tended so.

It takes a while, a diagnostic bent, patience, a fine eye. Medicine or writing. Keats and Conan Doyle. Or the obvious American example, William Carlos Williams, who, like Keats, chose poetry first. As remains the case in the UK, a medical degree in 1902 at the University of Pennsylvania was a fully undergraduate program. Williams was living in Penn's dorms, reading Keats, writing poems about castles, princes, chaste overwrought beauties lounging about, work he later admitted more than archaic, just plain awful.

However smitten by poetry, Williams did turn his eye to anatomy, chemistry, his hospital rotations, real ailments for some very physical figuring-out, when he wasn't fooling around on the violin or listening to Ezra Pound, his dormitory mate at Penn and even then fellow poet raving on about what was wrong with his work and most poetry, and—for god's sake, Willie!—those he should be reading night and day to call himself a writer at all. What about Yeats?—who had most dramatically arrived at Penn to present his poems in public, a visit Williams missed, to Pound's great disdain.

We're not far from Gary Stuart's soggy breadcrumb trail here, his thoughtful ways in our house. Williams eventually worked from hard observable image, his often repeated "no ideas but in things" against dreamy agenda and worn-out story. Even in high school, his very first poem broke, he said later, "a spell of disillusions and suicidal despondency" or just plain teen angst, Williams style, *diagnosed* by sharp observation. "A black, black cloud," he wrote, "flew over the sun / driven by fierce flying / rain." In his autobiography, he cherishes this scrap.

> The joy I felt, the mysterious, soul-satisfying joy that swept over me at that moment was only mitigated by the critical comment which immediately followed it. How could the clouds be driven by the rain? Stupid. But the joy remained. From that moment I was a poet.

Joy—is joy, and to be relished, at all costs. As for vivid clues—basement to second floor, and whatever storm involved—one is grateful. But how wildly important to American poetry—newly alive!—that *Stupid* in there, a refreshing get-a-grip on the self. It underscores a habit Williams later said he prized in the poems of others and hoped for in his own work: "the humility and caution of the scientist." *Rain* and *cloud* and *sun*, his first stab at channeling Adam in the garden, the delight in simply naming things.

In his early thirties, a decade of medicine behind him, came "Pastoral," destined for his first book.

114

When I was younger
it was plain to me
I must make something of myself.
Older now
I walk back streets
admiring the houses
of the very poor:
roof out of line with sides
the yards cluttered
with old chicken wire, ashes,
furniture gone wrong:
the fences and outhouses
built of barrel-staves
and parts of boxes, all,
if I am fortunate,
smeared a bluish green
that properly weathered
pleases me best
of all colors.

          No one
will believe this
of vast import to the nation.

This could be seen as pure privilege talking, but Williams makes clear his wonder, a credible start to any reassessment. Little is glorified though the fences of "barrel-staves / and parts of boxes" are beautiful, losing and gaining color in wind and rain. The mock-lordly shift in diction feels a little comic: "vast import to the nation." Or it's poking fun at the self to get out of self. That run of hard image means the immediate does count. "Nothing startles me beyond the moment," wrote Keats. Williams ends *as is*, not what-will-be or who's at fault.

What it *isn't* is poetry as ponderous, thousand-pound proclamation—fix your life or any life and here's how to do it—a danger inherent in this genre that lends itself to sanctimonious advice told by just another smart so-and-so who thinks he/she's been there. Instead, this speaker is witness to the world's rich layers: he's *just saying*. He isn't the village explainer though he walks through that village. Little things go vast. It's Keats,

Williams' first love, who relished "the . . . imaginative mind [that] may have its rewards in the repetition of its own silent working continually on the Spirit with a fine Suddenness—to compare great things with small." And Williams refusing the heavy-handed seems in line with Keats's emphatic "How we hate poetry which has a palpable design on us." Diagnosis, not treatment, not cure. This one opens to *humanity*. Poem as *knock knock, who's really there?*

Which should have been my own first question in the cadaver lab. In that room white as the blank page where the words *spinal cords* were magic-markered on plastic buckets, where fans whirled continuously, where four human beings lay in their final solitude; no, it was closer to Williams' *Stupid* in my inner ear. The ridiculous, sobering nerve of my standing there, my own body going abruptly strange in a kind of wonder or empathy. Some experiences return us to a first moment, all sides fallen away, ancient. Days and months, such primal looking was a profound *into*, the body a mysterious *given* and its *just wait*.

It's that wait that worries, rewards, blunt-questions greatly. Is this what poems and stories do? We *come to* in the looking, the writing, the reading. The patterns we imagine, half mirrored from life, half invented or mimed on the page. To diagnose includes Sherlock's "hundred little dodges," Conan Doyle tells us. Things add up. His detective *gathers* for whatever *ah-ha!* moment, the Rube Goldberg machine of the human brain first complicating A to B to C, the narrative drive. A "drop of water" might suggest "the possibility of an Atlantic or a Niagara without having seen or heard of one or another." The mind, through Robert Lowell's remote sensing, his great emptiness, *suggests* then delivers a drive up "the skull's hill." Images—hey, an idea just wants some company! Sherlock Holmes infers small bits from larger until all narrows again to *reasoned*, thus *reasonable*. It's also *if* and *then* for Conan Doyle, though probably not the same as Lowell's *if-in-the-middle-of-my-life-I-find-myself-in-a-dark-wood-aka-a-miserable-Peeping-Tom-to-callow-youth-parked-and-making-out-near-the-graveyard*, *then*, guess what? I'm worlds more troubled than I thought.

Trouble grows slowly in Conan Doyle's *A Study in Scarlet*, a novel that begins with genuine verve, his first literary effort to succeed, drafted in his Portsmouth surgery, a lot of time for that since his solo medical practice was a bust, and he wrote to his mother he was pretty much starving. In this first Sherlock Holmes story, we meet that intrepid narrator, John Watson, at work on his own diagnosis of who this odd duck might be, his new flat-mate Sherlock Holmes, and what he really does between bouts of depression and exuberant lab tests to distinguish fruit stains from blood stains.

Holmes is the real thing, brilliant undercover aider and abettor to save Scotland Yard idiots from themselves. Conan Doyle did in fact revolutionize forensics, put it on the map even. His detective keeps noting footprints in muddy yards to figure the height and weight of suspects, pauses at the victim's lips for the scent of poison, never *ever* jumps to conclusions. There are also Sherlock's more eccentric contributions to crime fighting, like his monograph on cigar ashes, their wit and wisdom and what they reveal.

Set in London, the first section is where the best writing lives. The novel's interminable second part should have kept it off the *Classic Comics* list, though I never got *A Study in Scarlet* in my Christmas stocking like the *Oliver Twist* and *Moby Dick* I found rolled up in there. Still, it *is* cartoon-like, that second section given over to the American West with a long, melodramatic gallivant in Mormon territory, circa 1860, complete with stick-figure bad-guy Latter Day Saints, threat and murder, our heroes hiding out in Utah's rocky beauty, a place the author had, naturally, never seen. It's startling how desperate a writer can get, his Mormon bashing just a bone thrown to cultural prejudice, clearly a lurid ploy to sell books. After all, the doctoring thing wasn't turning out that well. But how very bad his sentences can be at this point in the novel: "The sight of the fair young girl, as frank and wholesome as the Sierra breezes, had stirred his volcanic, untamed heart." Or "'Then mother's a deader too,' cried the little girl, dropping her face in her pinafore and sobbing bitterly."

I have to add that I first read this dreadful section on a British train from Edinburgh to Cornwall, dumbfounded though a little amused by his outrageous digression into my own country's western expanse, a place the author had never stepped foot. Outside, sheep were everywhere and uncountable, the rolling hills green and definitely English, and yes, lovely—lovely!—even as what I was reading went cardboard, into dimwitted new-world-frontier clichés. At last the narrative returns to England—wise move, better writing—and to Sherlock Holmes, busy all along in ways that show—he says so himself!—that "genius is an infinite capacity for taking pains."

Conan Doyle's old teacher, Joseph Bell, never fully comfortable with his widely proclaimed part in the main character's genesis, took his own pains, when interviewed, to round-about a little.

> I always impressed on my students—Conan Doyle among them—the vast importance of little distinctions, the endless significance of trifles. The great majority of people resemble each other in the main and larger feature . . . a head, two arms, a nose, a mouth, and a certain number of teeth. It is the little differences, in themselves trifles, such as the droop of an eyelid or what not, which differentiate men.

Diagnosis, the first step is one big no, not dehydration, not the thyroid, not MS. You *rule out*—*RO*, as doctors shorthand their notes. Joseph Bell later came up with this succinct gem: "the importance of the infinitely little is incalculable." Surely that's the upshot of these "trifles," these minute differences that point to an answer. Later, not exactly sidestepping a little immodest self-portraiture, Dr. Bell agreed his old student had, yes,

> created a shrewd, quick-sighted, inquisitive man, half doctor, half virtuoso, with plenty of spare time, a retentive memory, and perhaps the best gift—the power of unloading the mind of all the burden of trying to remember unnecessary detail.

That's another way to say it: *things to leave out.* Breaking news: we don't need to know everything. As to what makes Sherlock tick, Watson deliciously points out ways the detective does and does not keep lively and reachable. The man, he says, is "feeble" about literature, philosophy, astronomy, politics. Botany? "vari-

able but well up in belladonna, opium and poisons generally."
Anatomy: "accurate but unsystematic." Sensational literature:
"appears to know every detail of every homicide perpetuated in
the century." Accomplished violinist, boxer, swordsman. "Good
practical knowledge of British law."

In his own defense, the able Sherlock offers up this advice:

> A man should keep his little brain-attic stocked with all the
> furniture that he is likely to use, and the rest can be put away
> in the lumber-room of his library, as he can get to it if he
> wants to.

If he wants to—or is able. "In diseases," Keats wrote in his lab
notes, quoting his brilliant, sometimes skeptical teacher Astley
Cooper, "medical men guess. If they cannot ascertain a disease,
they call it nervous."

It's fair to say that Conan Doyle at his best does not succumb
to uncertainty or a shrug but reliably hones in through both
serious deductive reasoning and swift intuition, which is to say
logic *and* imagination. His detective in *A Study in Scarlet* looks
out the window at a figure headed toward his door, identifying
in seconds the man by gait and posture as retired Royal Navy.
Watson marvels at this "brain-attic" retrieval, to see *through* to
worlds unseen.

Where to go with this? Because after a few weeks of Monday,
Wednesday, and Friday mornings in the cadaver lab, I did be-
gin to figure out—get *context* for—what I would draw on Tues-
days and Thursdays, those fearless models in the studio quietly
posed amid the rush of so many pencils on paper, that hypnot-
ic, beautiful sound. Thanks to the cadaver lab, I could see the
tough muscle down to bone, the secret architecture within. An
informed trance as I drew, so like the descending, almost dis-
embodied concentration needed for poems, how to write them,
and their revision.

Lester King, a physician who thought deeply about medical
ideas (his book rightly titled *Medical Thinking*), doesn't mention
trance but insists that "a trace" in diagnosis—like an old TV still
in a fade after shutting down, or heat from a lamp clicked off—is

the most telling clue doctors track. For writers too, the terrible or endearing glow of an image keeps hanging around. *Knock knock* again. A trace? Who *was* there? Can you trace back? Conan Doyle calls his book *A Study in Scarlet*, copped from Sherlock's lordly remark to Watson: "a scarlet thread . . . runs through the colorless skein of our life, and our duty [is] to unravel it."

Poems often start in reverse too; those we read yesterday and long ago. I'm thinking Keats here, so smitten with Wordsworth, with Milton and Spenser, with Shakespeare above all, the moment he slipped sideways beyond them into high gear, his *traces* coming together in some stilled original moment of clarity. It's said he was walking from Hampstead back to London, thrilled by a recent meeting with poet Leigh Hunt, who had recognized his gift. He was twenty years old, a luminous something vague in his head until he got home to his flat to ink it all down—

> Much have I travell'd in the realms of gold,
> And many goodly states and kingdoms seen;
> Round many western islands have I been . . .

You might know the rest of this famous sonnet. Keats was no doubt calling down his own tragic or radiant traces—his mother's death, his work at Guy's Hospital, his dream of a trek through the Lake District then Scotland, his soon-to-be freedom from medicine, the fact of a planet, Uranus, newly named among stars, an ocean crossed by imagination many times—he'd been reading Robertson's *History of America*, a country, a continent largely unexplored, his Balboa and Cortez conflated. He was young. Early morning. He felt great. Chapman's new translation of Homer, what he and his old friend Charles Cowden Clarke had been reading that night, talking crazy until dawn, it flat-out astonished him—

> Then felt I like some watcher of the skies
> When a new planet swims into his ken:
> Or like stout Cortez when with eagle eyes
> He star'd at the Pacific—all his men
> Looked at each other with a wild surmise—

And maybe it wasn't TB. Maybe he'd live after all. But that's not exactly a premise.

God forbid, and Keats forgive me: a premise, perhaps leading to a proof. The "scientific method" is said to underlie diagnosis. The real nature of such horse sense? I ask my friend and colleague, linguist April Ginther, who rails in her usual passionate dismay at how that method is chronically misunderstood, even in the Academy.

Look-it, she says. A premise is an idea about something. Here's the thing: it's not your mission to prove it. You try things against it. You try to *prove your premise wrong.* That's the famous scientific method. In a nutshell. Go negative. Use whatever you can. If the notion survives, you're in business.

So you're right if you're wrong? I ask. About what might kill off your premise? To fail is to—not fail? April shrugs, in mock—maybe real—exasperation. *I'm not talking about failure,* she says.

But later that week I find myself in workshop telling my students, as if clear on this for a lifetime: Look, this is how revision works. This is our scientific method. Keep staring down your drafts, reading aloud, weighing each word. Throw every bell and whistle to undo it. Grrr! And great! Revision. To *resee.* I'm not talking about failure, I add.

Vaguely, only vaguely, do I know what's what. It does feel close to my daily discipline—my "hospital rounds" I call it—predawn visits with my poems-in-progress as if they are coma victims. I'm the well-meaning friend hanging around so if they rouse I will hear it: a new phrase, line, a change in tense. Me, a mere scribe poised to *rule out* or let live. I try to hold back. A poem finds its own shape.

Yet Euclid's premise-rich proofs; sonnet-like, aren't they? That ending turn, that *therefore Socrates is a fish* moment. Both sonnet and geometric proof are such human inventions; they ache and leap and try to make good on a promise. Okay, so Socrates was never much of a fish. But poetry is way less willed; writers are carpenters building image on image, a visible *surface,* however mysterious, through which lasting ideas might drift up, at best surprising the writer too. We make the *occasion* for meaning. And hope it works. *Premise?* I mean, what's with that *pre* in there—as if all's understood, in its proper place in advance.

One never knows at the start. Toward the end of my time in the dissection lab, I watched stunned as they removed the head from my favorite cadaver, a woman who, like her three compatriots, generously gave her body for such study. That head business, crucial because those doctors-to-be must see *into* the neck, most splendid conduit of high-speed traffic—all nerves, muscles, arteries—between brain and below. The medical student took some time with that saw. (Dear skull, I thought, it doesn't want to leave its body). Next to me stood a young man with whom I had spoken a lot. He seemed frozen too, just when we all assumed we'd mastered this art of observation, and acceptance, no matter what. "Sometimes," he said, "I really wonder what it's like in this room, I mean for someone from the outside." Then, after a pause that passed into prehistory as we watched his classmate bear down again and again: "I think this is one of those times."

Right, I said. A shared silence after that, gratitude and near-disbelief at the cadaver's unimaginable gift to us. And only the sound of the saw. Lester King, on medical thought, says it's not questions that alter over a week or a millennium, but the answers. And the way to those answers? The eye's still on that mouse in the dining room, but what of our remote-sensing device, the *wait, oh yeah*, which includes the racket out in the street? And that boiling pot of water in the next room dropped—or someone's about to drop it—hot-flooding the kitchen.

Aren't we still thinking about thinking here? John Hunter, that teacher of the teacher of Keats, wrote: *Don't think. Try!* And there's always one's humanity—*context*—to worry through. James Walker, the anatomist said: *identify, appreciate, move on.* And Grace Benedict, my drawing teacher: *look, think, make a mark.* Attention deepens slowly, both a scare and a solace. The body's troubles are evolutionary too, even in the short run. I saw in that lab how in a single life one nerve will cover for another, stricken bits will realign to self-repair but the complete *Where's Waldo?* mess in there is mainly high-minded. And no matter how fixed your eye might be on the model in life drawing class, the wily hand holding the pencil has its own ideas. Straight reasoning isn't the ticket. I suppose this makes medicine an art as well as a science. Nor do the click-clack blocks of logic work for poetry, though surely the ghost of the sonnet, its powerful turn of realization, is all over free verse to re-enact the most life-giving of our human habits. The whole mad affair so delicate, shouldn't the know-it-all in us be kept a muted thing? Poetry *is* the closest literary form we have to silence, and in that it could resemble pure thought.

What's a premise, anyway? Think of Bishop's first line, "the art of losing isn't hard to master," which she most brilliantly, with real wit, does disprove, the piece working like some perverse Euclidean proof, or—ditto—Phillip Larkin's "Always too eager for the future, we / Pick up habits of expectancy." And I suppose Roethke's confounding reversal at the start—*I wake to sleep and take my waking slow*—does begin an argument, then perhaps goes too dreamy for that. Always there's Keats's *This mortal body of a thousand days . . .* Which itself movingly proves how "but to think is to be full of sorrow." Because, count them: he *did* have only about a thousand days left. All right, a premise—a fortune telling, secret writing on the wall, the thing you go out whistling from a concert—could arrive anywhere in the poem or go stealth to low-jolt endlessly. This too: lyric or narrative progression can spook big time when it bears witness.

That progression can be playful too, frivolous as a set piece. In the archives at Surgeon's Hall in Edinburgh, one of the great surgical museums of the world, there's a little flip book Conan Doyle made, many small photographs bound, ready under any thumb to enact a tiny movie, rushed frame after frame: the writer lifting a blurred white-gloved hand to the brim of his hat coming forward and off as he smiles, eyes up to see—my god, where did it go?—the hat back, he's at the brim with that white-glove again—hello!—adjusting it properly dapper. A bauble, a goof. Conan Doyle in his glory years. He's having fun, he's made it, he's decades past his hardscrabble childhood in Edinburgh, his sad drunken father, his bad luck as a doctor. Chill out, Sherlock. Conan Doyle takes off his hat and puts it on, looking impish, a wave to us in the future. Easy! Is it? His intricate gestures slow down as you press back pages to release. There are poems as gracefully rendered as that flip book, the hat safely returned to a human head. Conan Doyle smiles again. Back to—maybe a nice lunch.

It could well be there's no clear premise in the world, that no reason and order or hats back on will save us or make for decent poems that pretend to. Still, if a new detail's revealed in this diagnostic process, an image or shift of voice derailing intention, throwing out the self-absorbed, the cloying and staid, the kneejerk said-a-zillion-times-until-it-means-nothing, then life becomes possible. How exactly is *my* mind "not right"? Mystery and its burdens. Rule in, rule out. A thought in the making *makes itself*, no matter how much time's involved, how many visits to the *will-the-poem-live?* coma ward. It's no longer personal, it's huge.

Yes. And no. It's just that the body is mortal and human attention is not; it keeps going. The same questions: more surprise? more depth? more unstoppable hunger? An old college boyfriend of mine liked to blurt out to anyone: *How do you get there? First, you go there!* For his part, Sherlock Holmes takes note of every little thing in the room. He stands there still, like a ticking clock. And Keats, he keeps walking back to London that morning, darkly ecstatic, writing, rewriting in his head. Diagnosis: you solve for *x*, what that real nightingale triggered. Williams wrote in his *Autobiography* how close these two worlds, poetry and medicine. "That is the poet's business," he said, "not to talk in vague categories but to write particularly, as a physician works upon a patient, upon the thing before him, in the particular to discover the universal."

That's near truism by now, a yawn, until you look into your own pages and see a bland welter of *so-what?* staring you down. Prove it! Diagnose! You're back to case history, to signs and symptoms. And image: how on earth does this poem *mean?* And get bigger?

No prediction, no cure, no trip-wired happy ending, but an inkling. The world might not end tomorrow. Think of that! Such quiet sets in before you write anything worthwhile, as it writes *you* into the next moment. I imagine it's like that long pause just after the invention of the stethoscope in the nineteenth century, maybe the first time in history—my god!—they *stopped talking*.

Breathe deep, she heard, and didn't know what to think. That weird new contraption against her chest was cold, it stung a little. Abruptly the doctor shut up too. He listened hard. He closed his eyes. They both leaned into it.

Three Blakes

Blake One

Finally it's not a dream. You plug in somewhere, to the long on-going. You read and read anything as a kid. After that, post-kid, it's more like cleaning out your great aunt's attic, surprised at the occasional treasure you find. Which leads back, like me at age nine or so, sitting up on the very high roof of a barn-turned-garage in Tuscola, the little Illinois town where my real Aunt Nell lived and died, looking down to the auction going on in her big side yard, all her *stuff*, this tall, scary woman who never much spoke to children. Now her life of things, strewn out on the grass.

My mother stepped up and took something off a card table. She was largely a speck from that altitude. And what she put into her bag, tiny. Much later, she passed it on to me: Aunt Nell's commemorative plate, marked 1914, 1915, then in French, *Glory to the Allies* with three crossed colorful flags glazed into it, a keepsake she received, a token to thank her because my great aunt had been there, driving an ambulance for the American Field Service in the First World War two years before we entered the fight.

I try to read that plate backwards now, to where and exactly who my Aunt Nell was when given such a thing early in the last century: a midwesterner, a small-town young woman inexplicitly there, driving through deep mud and ear-splitting gunshot somewhere near Paris. Was it innocence or experience or a curious suspension between those two states of being? Me, I was merely up on a roof, thrilled at the prospect: this place I would know all the summers of my childhood skewed at an angle, the adults I loved abruptly reduced, distracted with the minutiae of life after death. I got dizzy, forgotten up there, so secret. It's that secret thing when you read, isn't it? You and one poem. You found it. Or against all odds, it found you. You begin to lose balance, looking out over the great world.

Which is to say, of course I read William Blake in college. He was *assigned* for god's sake; I wrote a *paper* though my own time and place kept blowing up outside: Kent State a day's drive east, and now the National Guard patrolling our little college town. In this way, we mattered. In this way, he began to matter. Something edgy in the guy beyond the soothing rhythms of his day, his *Songs of Innocence* shuffled darkly to where *experience* holds court. A favorite: not the usual rose as iconic image but a promise: the world ravaged, or about to be.

> O Rose, thou art sick!
> The invisible worm
> That flies in the night,
> In the howling storm,
>
> Has found out thy bed
> Of crimson joy:
> And his dark secret love
> Does thy life destroy.

Really, isn't this heresy?—a classic beauty gone so viral that Sylvia Plath would find in her hospital bedside tulips the same toxic jolt some 170 years later. Just the bitten-raw nerve of rhyming "joy" and "destroy"; how close we are to Plath's dangerous flowers that "eat oxygen," her "dozen red lead sinkers around my neck." So even the lovely rose can go very bad indeed.

Blake's poem, "The Sick Rose," raves on, creature-odd and emblem-small, triggered by that first line's emphatic utterance, complete with exclamation point. Only two sentences, two abrupt quatrains cast off the mildly ecstatic "O," a habit of his day. Still, the poem didn't descend fully formed from clouds. In Blake's notebook, this draft has a significantly different ending:

> O Rose, thou art sick!
> The invisible worm

127

That flies in the night,
In the howling storm,

Has found out thy bed
Of crimson joy:
O, dark secret love
Doth life destroy.

To watch a mind unwork itself fascinates, makes human. In this early draft, a second exclamatory "O" underscores a larger mission beyond an eco-reality-check informing a rose of its fate (beware the worm's appetite!) or a schoolmarm's coded warning about sex (did I say "worm"? Well, you know what I said). More dire, it's love, the most obsessive kind destroying life itself, a thought upending our smiley expectations about love. But that second "O" marks it closer to melodrama, the poet loving his own voice aloft in summary proclamation.

Blake will make two small alterations that *remean*. In the final draft, he drops that second jacked-up "O." And though continuing to look into the sun for an eternal principle, he stays loyal to the originating I-thou approach: isn't this still just some worrywart out to warn a rose? But flowers can be killed this way, can be prey to whatever creatures. It's a grounding assumption that happens to be true. "And his dark secret love / does thy life destroy," he insists. Here the possessive pronoun *thy*—archaic even in Blake's time—keeps the progression personal, dialing down the grandiose. The poem remains intimately focused: a rose, targeted by direct address, to be stunned into red alert.

Things don't get better. We might warily cheer for a personified flower this oblivious as the predatory worm makes its unfathomable way in. The shifting sleight-of-hand is verb-driven. First a worm that "flies in the night" scares, the present tense making all so ongoing and unstoppable. But it's way worse, this thing most feared already hunkered down: "The invisible worm" . . . / Has found out thy bed / Of crimson joy: / And his dark secret love / Does thy life destroy." *Has found out.* Blake's suggestion of past tense is *experience* at work, and even that auto-stab at lulling rhyme—*joy* unto *destroy*—can't solace much. But his "destroy" is a turn to immediacy again, an endless *right now* that reaches into past and future. The voice-over voice is an urgent stage whisper: get out while you can. But guess what? You can't.

Auden says somewhere that as readers of poems, we *overhear* everything. I've been smitten by this notion many times: poem as retrieval device, as remote sensor of the hidden, perhaps unspeakable thoughts uttered to self or to the dead, or for one other before the world gets nosy, i.e., strangers, we who listen in. The stricken rose remains in our back vision, a worm burrowing there, the "howling storm" not far behind. But the thing *overheard.* The nerve of our being there at all! This very weird exchange unsettles because in spite of Blake's rhetorical flourish, it's so entirely *not* public; the extended metaphor is going private, about to spring. It's human love too, an equation we make via a slow interactive *gulp.* It settles inside us. Be warned.

This turn from all-is-well to pure chill has a much larger life in Blake's work, a clue to the overall structure of his *Songs of Experience,* in which "The Sick Rose" is one thrilling part. The basic premise is a before-and-after slide show, the first move an upswing we hear even in the Rose poem's initial "O," a brief homage to beauty itself before the inevitable derangement: *Songs of Innocence and Experience.* The drill on that: two parts, *Innocence* published first in 1782, reprinted five years later with its *Experience* attached, a joined thing, a progression, howbeit a stained one. His naïve semisweet ragas lead. But get real: the world is sorrow and injustice. Blake offers up a whole set of poems to prove that more dire take, and more of them too.

At twenty, new to the sequence, I stepped back and even now: what an astonishingly simple idea, an architectural expanse of so many flickering bits. Because these *Songs* do make a loose sequence, a flip book, a near-Muybridge sweep rendered in stills. Time passes and passes until it's hope unto disaster, a darker complication, even into the street where cheerful enough then very troubled citizens speak up for themselves: a poor chimney sweep, the nurse, a little girl headed into terrible straits, that era of bread riots, a Napoleonic war, typhus and TB, early death. This downward curve—bad stuff *is* inevitable—may be a familiar, life-lesson plot, half *duh!* to those of us who write and read under our beloved black visors. Still it assaults, and surprises.

The shape holds up. Blake's design *resembled* the year I found him too, 1970 and its swift transitions, our hanging around young and as brilliantly empty as that rose, amazed at the soldiers and their tanks coming down the street to quell a "student riot," our just standing there trying hard to be amused, nervously joking—classes were cancelled—until the bull-horned threats, the warning shots in air. Then we were running, the smell of chemicals, something burning, and it smarted, our eyes tearing up. *Smarted.*

Experience, a definition: a past tense that sticks but you go back until it vanishes. It's now, present tense, all the *what was* evoked and here it comes, innocence once more but twisted there, a shadow. What does it taste like? It tastes like those chemicals.

Think of Blake, his transformation in flight, poems of innocence *and* experience, that *and* again like they're equal, or that they mean something bigger because they're juxtaposed. His before and after, expansion and contraction at it and at it because poems and even stories lie outside of time and make an unearthly ruckus. Or there's a question Blake keeps asking under those songs: which is better, not knowing or knowing, the future or the past, to dream or to remember that dream? Which is sadder? And which is truer? But poems take place between these two states of being, our dropping innocence into an elixir to become a thing altered on the page. *Smarted.* Not that it's smart. It just stings.

So this is the first Blake I offer. How from a roof, a side yard opens to a battlefield in France, the old suddenly new in such smoke. Or it's a report, a shot out of hell in whatever college town. Then it's a fuse smothering dim, a bright burn in hiding. You wonder, who *is* this guy, this poet? Though his face remains curiously gentle in the pictures that survive, his pale head hovering moon-like in any biography's glossy insert, he gets quarrelsome. His fiery, measured take on things might suffice—if you are young enough—to pull you away from the necessary it-is-always-thus melodrama of being young: who am I, who will I love, what in the world to do with this life? Old enough, those questions still at us, we're stopped short by Blake forcing a look at this thing "innocence" against what "experience" might mean. Take note again: he chose that "a" word, innocence *and* experience. A leveling, an attempt at parity to stave off the worst, sure.

Remember Elizabeth Bishop: her "everything only connected by 'and' and 'and'." But it's confusing and dangerous too. Just a thought, said the lamb to the lion, in all innocence.

Blake Two

In fact, he wasn't a poet, not mainly or much. So assumed many in his own day, surprised if not dismissive that he wrote at all, this William Blake the engraver, occasional painter, hardscrabble printer with reliable technical chops.

Not a poet perhaps, but definitely peculiar, first inklings of that from his father, a mildly successful hosier, a devout Christian, albeit a "dissenter" with radical religious and political views in Britain's rigid class system. In 1772, after learning to draw and copy accurately in Henry Pars' drawing school on the Strand, Blake saved the family money by not going on to art school, apprenticed instead at fifteen to James Basire, an antiquarian engraver both disparaged and respected for his old methods with line, his close observation of tiny "particulars," never an apostle of the muzzy, more romantic mezzotint coming into vogue. That throwback preference was Blake's too for what he called "the historic class" of artists, Michelangelo and Durer, their direct muscular approach to the ideal human figure in those prints he'd collected since childhood. Rubens? Blake despised such flashy ultra-decorative looseness from the start.

It helped that he never got along with the other apprentices in the shop, though it wasn't really punishment but a kind of shrewd "time-out" that Basire kept sending him back alone to make drawings in Westminster Abbey, later to be engraved, months unto years his wandering its ghostly rooms among the gothic eternity-bound sculpture. He would climb on the tombs, look down and meticulously reproduce on paper how those oversized figures of kings and queens and who-knows-who-else slept stone-still for centuries as ornament and icon on each sarcophagus.

As much as he saw, he saw *beyond* and *back* to an earlier time: monks in long lines, chanting their plainsong, swinging their censers. He'd been a fearless witness of visions starting at four,

131

claiming that the face of God had appeared in his window, the family's house built on a very old graveyard, Pesthouse Close, which gave off an unsettling stench—proof!—when it rained. Then that tree full of angels when he was nine, walking home, minding his own business. Later, more angels standing inexplicably among the threshers in fields as if that were perfectly natural. In keeping with his own strict discipline in drawing, he insisted, "A spirit is not a vision, not a cloudy vapor but organized and minutely articulated." The years at Westminster sealed his love and wonder before the ancient and archaic, the stark and the strange.

At twenty-two, his apprenticeship ended; he did nerve up and apply to the distinguished Royal Academy, admitted pointedly as an "engraver," an art form written off as a thing of mere commerce. As such, he could only be an "associate" of the school, never a full-fledged student. Blake took a painting class and a course called "Perspective," then anatomy taught by William Hunter, whose brother John—a physician and also an anatomist—founded London's remarkable Hunterian Museum and was the teacher of the teacher of Keats when he studied medicine at Guy's Hospital some decades later. In the Royal Academy class, the student artists drew the cadavers of criminals propped up, reeking to high heaven. Working that way was a "hateful" experience "smelling of mortality," Blake is said to have said. Instead he kept his eye fixed on the old artists he loved—so unfashionable then—their sketches and paintings and sculpture.

At the Academy, much distressed him and built that chip on his shoulder, the clash of taste and class, the condescension he felt. He detested its celebrated director, the urbane, articulate portrait painter Joshua Reynolds, the darling of wealthy patrons, paid unthinkable sums for his work. Blake's margin annotations on Reynolds' *Discourses* underscore his take on the man:

REYNOLDS: I felt my ignorance, and stood abashed.
BLAKE: A Liar, he never was Abashed in his Life & never felt his ignorance. . . .
REYNOLDS: But this disposition to abstractions . . . is the great glory of the human mind.

BLAKE: To Generalize is to be an Idiot To Particularize is the Alone Distinction of Merit— General Knowledges are those Knowledges that Idiots possess.

He did show paintings in the Academy's galleries—an honor to be chosen—but always watercolors since he passionately disliked oils (Reynolds' specialty, by the way): too muddy, not to be trusted, and *the* method in that period which would have certainly set the cantankerous Blake right off. Resistance, of course: the ground-zero stance in all his work. Everything about him conflicts, his painting exuberant and severe at once. "Thou readest black when I read white," he wrote, even about the Bible. But method there too. "Without contraries there is no progression," must be his most revealing and often quoted directive.

Then and ever after was the dangerous, acid-toxic trade he knew by trial and error and by heart: the engraving, and his lackluster business smarts at that. "For better or worse, for a Period of Forty years," he wrote about himself in 1809, "he never suspended his labours on Copper for a single Day." Continually on the edge of financial ruin, he made books and pamphlets (most demeaning—no matter his earnings from it very late in life—that he engraved the catalogue for the Wedgewood China Company catalogue). But some of that work mattered to him. He inked and etched, printed and bound, adding color to his daring line drawings in service to writers living and dead, sometimes the great among them–Thomas Gray, Milton, Dante, Tom Paine. A life of 580 copper plates, the ones we can track.

Regardless, his poems kept coming, and after his first collection—*Poetical Sketches*, knockoffs of Milton and Spenser brought out by a friend—he printed his own books, a literal *thingness* to them, the words' smallest heft built up with glue, a laborious, very physical method—"relief etching"—he claimed his beloved dead brother Robert taught him in yet another vision. As Allen Ginsberg would say two centuries later: Blake used his "whole intelligent body" to make that work. Never just lines on a page, first and last for Blake was the drawn-and-seen image, crucial to the words. But never many copies. Shockingly few—just twenty-seven of his conjoined and illustrated *Songs*— have come down to us. Of the later prophetic works, *Jerusalem* for example, only one, and of his *Marriage of Heaven and Hell,* a whopping five originals exist.

And no, not illustrated, in fact, *illuminated,* as richly embellished as any book of hours eked out by monks in the ninth century—a tradition Blake willfully tapped—shot through with light not of this earth. Considered now the most brilliant colorist of that period, he cut in whitening and carpenter's glue for a thick watercolor mix, a secret he claimed St. Joseph shared in a vision. Three layers' worth, finish up with a varnish over the whole lot. It still glows! (Case in point: years ago in the Philadelphia Museum of Art, I came around a corner. I know now that genius hits without a name to alert you. Before I had any idea of *what,* right there: a small intricate square, dazzling and eye-level. 1792, his "Nativity" a startling, surreal take on the classic Madonna and child motif which has the divine infant leaping out of Mary who sinks back against Joseph, the small figure spun out, propelled across the room, aimed at St. Elizabeth's open arms, and on her lap another tiny boy, John the Baptist, legendary witness of the birth. A flying baby! How gloriously weird is that? He must have lowered his brush thinking *not bad, this might do.* As for my own small moment; was that even thinking, to be set adrift like that?)

So, Blake, not really a poet? Because most writers alive then missed him by design or by ignorance, the younger Keats and Shelley included. The rest: one wrote that "he has made several irregular and unfinished attempts at poetry." Another called him "an eccentric lunatic." And Robert Hunt, critic-most-feared: "whatever license we allow him as a painter, to tolerate him as a poet would be insufferable." So much for the poetry police at their blackballing blood sport, then and always thus, I suppose. A very public comeuppance though: flash forward two hundred years to the preface he discarded for his long poem "Milton," which included a small untitled lyric known these days as "Jerusalem" (distinct from his epic of that name), the cherished hymn sung as the triumphant finale of *The Proms* with its memorable "England's green and pleasant land," though it famously condemns Britain's mills as "satanic" just before these lines ring out—

Bring me my Bow of burning gold;
Bring me my Arrows of Desire;
Bring me my Spear: O clouds unfold:
Bring me my Chariot of Fire.

In his own time, the jury was still out, the few on it anyway. Charles Lamb dismissed Blake as "a mad Wordsworth"; surely some praise there. As for the resolutely *unmad* great man of the period, Wordsworth did throw Blake a bone, admitting the *Songs* had some "elements of poetry—a thousand times more than either Byron or Scott." His margin notes: "there is no doubt this man is mad but there is something about this madness I enjoy." One poet embraced him: Coleridge, considered a bit daft himself but perhaps sweetened, made wiser by his own opium dreams, even seeking out Blake for a meeting, a calm and mutually savored time spent. "Congenial beings of another sphere, breathing for a while on our earth" as one Charles Augustus Tulk observed. Imagine their afternoon. Such pleasure! As for our time, I leave it to John Berryman, whose *Dreamsongs* owe him a lot. "I don't contradict madmen," he said in a *Paris Review* interview. "When William Blake says something, I say thank you."

And always the *Songs* themselves growing stubbornly as innocence does into experience, slowly as one's writerly chops kick in, to embolden. Or as quickly, everything jelling almost overnight when you thought you were just sleeping. Some came early, as in Blake's *An Island in the Moon*, an unlikely satire, talking heads arguing philosophy, science, and art, a play with characters of smart-ass charm with names like "Inflammable Gass" and my personal favorite, "Obtuse Angle" ("who understood better with his eyes shut"), singing a version of "Holy Thursday" and "Nurse's Song."

It's the Note Book though, belonging first to his much mourned younger brother Robert, that served as Blake's totem and worry stone until his death, scribbled and overscribbled, the main source for the drafts, many largely unchanged when added to the *Songs* like "The Clod & the Pebble" or "The Garden of Love" or the only slightly revised "Christian Forbearance" morphed more damning in its new title, "A Poison Tree." Just the standard MO for a guy whose last patron, John Linnell, considered him "a saint amongst the infidels and a heretic among the orthodox." (Think of the Note Book's *Nobodaddy* pieces, his name for the first person of the Trinity he wrote off as tyrannical, and mocked as such.) His revising kept on. Perhaps to echo *Innocence*'s "Infant Joy" and its couple of quatrains, Blake radically altered the Note Book's "Infant Sorrow" in the *Experience* version: two stanzas, down from seven. Was it partly the illustration—no, the *illumination*—and what space was left for words once Blake cut into the copper plate the suffocating bedding and drapes, the child's arms raised in hysterical dejection, the mother bending to him?

> My mother groan'd! my father wept.
> Into the dangerous world I leapt:
> Helpless, naked, piping loud:
> Like a fiend hid in a cloud.

> Struggling in my father's hands,
> Striving against my swaddling bands,
> Bound and weary I thought best
> to sulk upon my mother's breast.

This revision must have been a painful but exacting negotiation between Blake the artist and Blake the poet, the visual imagery forcing the poet's *less* to mean *more*. Gone!—those "Priests by day / underneath the vines / like Serpents in the night." Gone!—the talk of "gore" and Blake's emo-editorial raving against the Church, his eye on the infant now who chooses "to sulk upon my mother's breast" given "the dangerous world." A straight shot, á la his apprentice days when Basire demanded a steely focus in those dark passageways at Westminster. The child's first utterance, "My mother groan'd," earns a sudden and suddenly poignant exclamation point: *My mother groan'd!* This most emphatic baby crying out is nothing like the child in *Innocence*'s "Infant Joy" who blithely sings "I have no name" and "Joy is my name / Sweet joy befalls me!"

Blake began his *Songs of Experience* keen for an honest pushback against the first and happier songs, his subtitle for the combined version a trumpet in that gloom—a "Shewing the Two

Contrary States of the Human Soul"—which goes beyond the standard religious read of a simple dichotomy after a fall from grace. This push-me/pull-me that marks progression became Blake's mantra. Or it was partly self-defense. He had a vision once of Satan under a walkway grate near his house, a face seething under metal bars, and called for his pen because "the fit of song was upon him," so his wife Catherine reported. Threat—no matter how linked to imagination—can exhaust itself. But maybe relief is threat in reverse, and carries similar power: "There's always a moment in the day Satan cannot find," he wrote, clearly a great weight off, or at least the terror under that grate erased for a while.

Sometimes this double life is visible on the page, a tonal holiday—or a dissonance—between Blake's drawings and the words they serve, where the former "illustrates" but separate lives are led. In his "The Garden of Love," the priests look duly pious in Blake's drawing though they are treacherous creatures "Binding with briars, my joys and desires," and that so-called "garden of love" is "filled with graves." Just as *The Tyger*'s wondrous "fearful symmetry" laid out, in theory, so orderly, with—well—symmetry, is rendered by a panicked run of questions: "What the hammer? what the chain? / In what furnace was thy brain?" How to understand the unvicious looking tiger-on-Prozac drawn below those words? It's that rousing up-yours of American poetry decades later: "Do I contradict myself? Then I contradict myself!, I contain multitudes." That would be Whitman, of course, who some say read Blake and loved Blake; others that he never or if he did, couldn't let on and threaten his own up-from-nowhere reputation for originality, though thinking ahead, trying to be practical, he seems to have designed his own mausoleum straight off Blake's famous engraving "At Death's Door," which shows a bent old man entering his final place of rest. But Whitman and Blake were destined for comparison, Swinburne later insisting that each was "coherent to himself, as strange without and as sane within." And Blake's contemporary, William Hazlitt, had this to say about that poet's perspective, how "it must be to a god" to whom "a worm crawling in a privy is as worthy an object as any other." Perhaps not fully the praise for Blake we might hope, but Hazlitt's take rings true for Whitman too.

The very act of engraving mimes this law of opposing energy that obsessed Blake as a rush forward, the two sides aching toward one that makes all things abruptly *meta*, the hard work of that printing process. That engravers learn to cut and build letters and images *backwards* so they come out right under the inked rollers must have daunted and pleased him. Or that Blake, forced by his necessary frugality, merely turned over the copper plates previously etched for *Innocence*, using that blank side to incise the *Experience* songs by the "graver," the name for both the tool and the one who knows to use it. Then the same buildup of glue, the bath of poisonous acids for innocence and experience equally, however opposite.

As in most plans, the idea went weirder in the making and departed from strict intention. Not all of Blake's *Songs* are equal and opposite; some stand alone, or connect by a trace. Some— like "Little Girl Found" which ends rather happily in *Experience*— carry their conflicting double within. That's crucial too: surprise, variation, digression, sudden flight. But the printing itself, how many shillings available for ink and paper, what colors for paint, the many times Blake fed the press and Catherine pulled pages into the window's light, their cheap one room or two rooms, a bed, a table, a couple of chairs, the awful fumes of it continually, the aprons and the inked mess, stray pencil erased with fistful of bread, but the reds and blues and yellows grew delicate, more radiant as he figured the measure, the weight, how much whitening and glue for each illumination as years passed, as they aged, London outside with its stink and its roar and its pounding injustice that made Blake write of the chimney sweep's blackened and body-broken misery twice, unthinkable even in innocence, his rage at the wife beater in the street, at the father who tied his boy's ankle to a heavy log and sent him off, Blake's furious words that stopped both. But the city's great quiet at times, and where he and Catherine walked along the Thames and out where sheep grazed and dotted the fields to make distance: imagine that too. It's a still, a set of stills like the *Songs* themselves, each moment of that process childless, full-up, a shared hard life-in-motion. Always new on some level as they lifted each page to see what it took off the copper, if image and words and the inking went right, it must have, the beauty, so much of it in that small room, an offering to something. Catherine Blake, who rarely seemed to leave her husband's side, is often quoted: "I have very little of Mr. Blake's company, he is always in Paradise." This must be a guide in any Blake-warm flood, the found Blake and lost Blake, the bewilderment of Blake. He saw things there and not-there, unlikely a matter of will. His visions—no, those *spirits!*—of course, of course, they *came to him*, as is said of such things. In addition to the centuries-old artists he loved—Raphael, Michelangelo among them—and his long-under-the-sod brother, he reported regular chats with Shakespeare, with young Milton, old Milton, with Dante; the sun itself once spoke to him. He said that visions often started his poems, like the piper who brings on the *Songs of Innocence* with his "rural pen" that "stain'd the water clear." He widened this notion, writing that all our fears and our hopes are just that: visions. Let that sink in, believe it briefly: *all fears, all hopes, are visions.* I don't know if that comforts or troubles, like I don't know, as a cradle Catholic gladly lapsed to a blank slate, quite how to begin each poem I write, to put on my "considering cap" as Blake liked to call it, to lift in some new way the veil he thought nothing of lifting, the one between present and past, the living and the dead, innocence and experience, between here and now, that bare slip of human energy that moves *no* to *yes.* So it is, what must be the key to poems; and at the rapt still heart of narrative's move through time, the lyric impulse there too, the lasting part of any story.

You could throw in the word "surreal" to pass these spirits off as invention, or revisit madness as Blake-stained, Blake-earned in the end. But to *see* things, though not entirely like Michelangelo, who claimed he found "the angel in the marble and carved until I set him free." It goes beyond that, to see *into* and no longer what you thought. Take a long, steady look at his paintings, their unimaginably wild life, bodies triumphant, often naked, rushing or stock-still in descent or ascension, the heroic everything-about-them in shocking color, sacred imagery gone profane, which is to say innocence passing through experience until so furiously innocent again. That's a reversal in the poems too, our inheritance. And first a pause, a real place where one is stripped down to knowing nothing and expecting nothing. "I can look at a knot of wood until I am frightened by it," Blake wrote.

So the timeless equation, poet equals *seer*, isn't only a matter of public pronouncement, his "Hear the voice of the Bard / who Present, Past and Future sees" that begins one of the songs. Such a big voice goes deeply interior too, off a lived life, to rattle understanding itself. Those spirits: it's one thing to have a loved lost one or a long ago hero appear out of nowhere in a dream or near-dream; that lies within mystic tradition, or ordinary deep-down wish to see mother/father/brother/beloved cousin again.

But Blake is way out there, much stranger. I think the most astonishing conversation of those he claimed to have had was not with the human dead. As he sat for his own portrait once, Blake spoke in the most matter-of-fact, this-reminds-me way of the angel who Michelangelo often drew, that artist's favorite model for the fresco as certainly the one both he and Michelangelo saw, howbeit centuries apart, and talked to, who talked back. It's scary and it's charming and what in the world to do with that? And who do any of us become that split-second we take such a vision as sure, what the hell, why not?

Blake Three

in which there is a dinner in Philadelphia, many springs ago, the Associated Writing Programs' annual meeting still small enough that everyone attending could fit into one room and raise a spoon and a glass. But that last evening would astound us, a promise I half-believed, that we'd be "entertained" at the conference center. Who would do that for us, and to us? I didn't have my program. I remember our table not too far from the front.

The Fugs! someone stage-whispered. The *what?* I flashed on their lyrics from the 60s which unnerved senselessly on purpose: *I want all of your skin, all of your skin!* my brother had loved to sing-shock to no one in particular, our mother passing through the kitchen, a collateral target. *Old* Fugs! They loped in, bony and regal as wolves, their graying hair shredded to confetti, moving toward us with guitars and their ultimate cool, then last—are you kidding me?—Allen Ginsberg in his Old Testament patriarch get-up: flowing white smock, what was left of his hair long, his beatific just-wait snarl as they stood in the empty center of our rafted-up tables. Right before us! No one spoke, nary a fork lifted. We'd been there years, right? permanently startled by this *visitation*, no other word for it. A vast, visible quiet—one *sees* quiet like that—and out of our staring, their staring back: a noise, they made a pure and sudden Blake noise, roaring into the *Songs of Innocence* and *Experience* to that other world where real poems live, able to make the impossible leap of two centuries. Songs terrible, beautiful, unruly. These guys, singing them! I don't know much more. The word *outrageous* will never quite do, so moved, so touched to the core, everyone I saw. High praise then, out of silence our tearing up, our laughter or nearly weeping, that line crossed and recrossed, who knew exactly? And Blake himself, abruptly off the page.

Where he must have been lurking all along, letting loose his own experience and innocence as honest-to-god songs in that posh London parlor turned literary salon of one very bluestockinged Mrs. Mathew, this most contrary Blake not yet thirty, before his "unbending deportment" was "not at all time considered pleasing," as a guest there later tactfully put it. *Before* means he kept singing, was "listened to by the company with silence, and allowed by most of the visitors to possess original and extraordinary merit," someone else remembered, an experience that got fictionalized and bravadoed up in a piece Blake wrote later in third person where a young man performing one of the *Songs of Innocence* is met by fifteen minutes of stunned, appreciative not-a-word.

We will never know his melodies for "The Chimney Sweeper" or "Nurse's Song" because Blake "wanted the art of noting it down," it was said. As solitary as he was, he apparently sang for friends too, maybe in lowbrow, comforting pubs, never far. And think of all the other sweet, rioting tunes he heard there; they sing-songed him good, if his own uncomplicated rhythms and rhymes on the page are any evidence.

It was Handel too, London opera-mad, though Blake was

not. Still, people talk: to have singer after singer change tone but not character, the aria a kind of mask. All poems are masks, Yeats said and Pound said, the former maybe the first poet to love Blake completely. In opera though, the *masque* is a throat, chest, space-in-the-head thing, how the voice gets made in the body's secret places, released as rich air into thin air. One sings through that masque to show time passing, changed circumstance, a many-layered *story* delivered in passionate bits. Robert Burns wrote songs too, ghostly soliloquies in his own and others' voices, political poems rising up, never allowed to be sung before. They drifted down from Edinburgh to London, ringing out in pubs and drawing rooms, so maybe Blake heard those and heard those, and heard those. . . . Influence: what a curious half-conscious mess of dumb want and accident, envy, admiration, even disdain. Under that is the numb fury all writers know: to make a thing disturbing and freshly shaped. What's harder– to keep it going.

How exact one *can* order the many and conflicting came to Blake to be distilled brand-new in his *Songs*, and that continues to come. American composer William Bolcom, inspired by the poet and equally unquiet, wrote his version, a three-hour masterwork begun in his teens and completed some forty years later. Blake's poems, Bolcom tells us in the CD's liner notes in 2004, are "exercises in Drydensque diction placed cheek to jowl with ballads that could have come from one of the 'songsters' of his day (small popular pamphlets of words set to well-known tunes)." Inviting singers with wildly varied approaches, Bolcom dreamed up different arrangements and musical styles for his adaptation, defying category or careful to include them all. In this way, he quite consciously invoked Blake's principle of opposing energies for genuine progression. "Cheek to jowl"—absolutely! A sample of what Bolcom's 450 performers brought to life: a country-western version of "The Shepherd," a Renaissance madrigal as the baseline for "Laughing Song," an electrifying reggae twist on "The Divine Image," ratcheting up Bob Marley to hell and back, "The Tyger" a near spoken-word piece thunder-chanted by a vast chorus to bone-chilled drumming, while "The Fly" is sung eerily by the sweetest children's choir imaginable. Though there are poignant torch songs against big band swing, or something achingly one-guitar-simple as in both nurse's songs, many pieces required a voice trained for opera, the tunes atonal or melodic, their major and minor turns backed by the orchestra in which our son—a student in Ann Arbor then—played cello as my husband and I watched spellbound from the balcony in the enormous Hill Auditorium at Michigan where Bolcom taught for years. The profound otherness—*from each other* too—of the songs themselves, poem-plus-poem, their abrupt and changing life and story fevered, solaced: all of it took hold for me. Blake as pure trance; get it? Trance means sequence: *keep it going*. Meaning: *I never want to leave*. And *why would I? The whole world is here*.

Indeed, as they say in the UK. And Blake's world is a matter of ongoing parts, gritty-political and public, though its speakers, persona or not, come off as deliciously then painfully private, in innocence or experience. In Ginsberg's *Howl*, we watch those passing "through universities with radiant cool eyes hallucinating . . . Blake-light tragedy among the scholars of war." *Blake-light*, then. A particular kind of "tragedy." A stay against confusion, Frost said of poetry, his lightning-quick analogy re-said in his name a million times, plus this time but Blake's *stay* keeps flickering in a most worldly confusion. Via meticulous craft—alliteration, fierce or quiet repetition, in shifting syntax that mimes thought itself by way of question and cool statement, heated exclamation—what we absorb is the explosive sound of London's public life and its interior spaces too.

"Daily intimate speech" and "talk-tones" is how Ginsberg explains much of Blake's diction and *duende*, citing his own visionary attempts "to tune" the *Songs* to match "each holy and magic syllable . . . as if each had intention." Begun the two weeks following what he called the "Democratic Convention 1968 Tear Gas Chicago," his putting music to Blake's poems was in part a matter of his learning chord changes on an old pump organ, major to minor most "appropriate particularly." Ezra Pound wrote that all art is made of a fixed element against a variable, another shift that feels a lot like Blake relishing his one-against-one. *Listen to the sound it makes*, Pound said. Bolcom's take on the poem "London," for instance, was richly informed by singer

Nathan Lee Graham, and though perhaps not quite how Blake would have belted it out in 1792, if rage and grief have a sound, surely both composer and performer have been especially alert to what the poet wrote.

> I wander thro' each chartr'd street,
> Near where the chartr'd Thames does flow,
> And mark in every face I meet
> Marks of weakness, marks of woe.
>
> In every cry of every Man,
> In every Infant's cry of fear,
> In every voice, in every ban,
> The mind-forg'd manacles I hear.
>
> How the Chimney-sweepers cry
> Every black'ning Church appalls;
> And the hapless Soldier's sigh
> Runs in blood down Palace walls.
>
> But most thro' midnight streets I hear
> How the youthful Harlot's curse
> Blasts the new born Infant's tear,
> And blights with plagues the Marriage hearse.

Bolcom's and Graham's apt handling here brings out what Ginsberg saw in Blake, savage turns of key, each syllable and its "holy"—howbeit unholy—intention underscored in his line breaks, the singer's long stress and rise on "every face I meeeeet," his "every Maaaan," and the poem's last sung word "hearse" delays the inevitable in a terrifying downward slur. Blake's hatred of all injustice, his distrust of the military (in spite of his empathy for the "hapless" soldier), his distaste for the Church and his feel of general doom, all nailed down tight by present tense and the steady, unforgiving four-beat line; one *hears* this as a physical assault. The repetition of "every"—*every* Man/cry/voice/ban, and later, "*every* black'ing church"—increases the burden on this speaker observing the city *right now*. That final line's fade and Nathan Graham's pauses between the phrases "and blights" and "with plagues" and "the Marriage hearse" bring home the think-again weight of closure itself. Bolcom's heavy metal decision to let electric guitar licks and drum invade that final stanza adds threat and chill. "These are perfect verses," Ginsberg wrote about Blake's words themselves, "with no noise lost, or extra accents for nothing." And Bolcom: "I have tried my best to *make everything clear* . . . the same way Blake used line and color, in order to illuminate the poems." Bolcom again: the work is "a series of arches, in both subject and emotions, each inhabiting a spiritual climate and progressing even further into it 'Shewing the Contrary States of the Human Soul.'"

A sequence begins as a narrative impulse, or a hoarder's sweet troubling dream: too much stuff to handle in a single lyric shot or two. That Blake keeps it simple through accumulation and the charm of a seemingly easy contrast is brilliant, because it misleads. "Contrary States" doesn't necessarily mean only two. The sequence gets unbelievably complex; its power lies in each song's unique and startling strangeness. The poet himself kept rearranging the furniture, some pieces first in *Innocence*, then raised up—or lowered—into *Experience*. Or returned to *Innocence* again, as Mapquest will tell step by step how to follow the bread crumbs back home or out into the great world. The more one stares into the *Songs*, the more unabsolute they feel: less happily-ever-after, that innocence, and certainly less damning that experience, just more dark amazement lost to wonder. How does it end? It doesn't.

Like it never ends in the Lake District where Wordsworth once lived at Dove Cottage and Coleridge made long visits, where Dorothy Wordsworth kept her remarkable journal that reveals so much of the underside of that era, where Keats walked the hills and later Hopkins too and maybe every other English poet worth his salt crackers and boots and hand-sewn notebook, a custom and a fashion, such wanderlust. It was there in little Grasmere a few springs ago where I'd taken the train down from Edinburgh to see the UK's Carol Ann Duffy, Scotland's Liz Lockhead, and Gillian Clarke of Wales, the three British Laureates read their poems at St. Oswald's, whose graveyard still guards what's left of the poet who did admit that Blake had "elements of poetry" in him. Afterwards, I stayed at the old church a few minutes, reading stone plaques built right into the wall. Below the pipe organ, the words on one completely stopped me:

> Dedicated to the Glory of God and in loving memory
> of Nellie Taylor, VAD, British Red Cross, of the 10th Motor
> Ambulance Convoy, who died in France, June 27th,
> 1916. . . . This Organ is the gift of her sorrowing parents.

My mother was a Taylor. Her aunt was Nell, my great aunt whose everything-she-owned had been laid out on the grass at that auction years ago when I looked down and thought myself a brave little kid, a secret up there on the barn roof. I read the plaque over and over, remembered the plate my aunt had been given, its glazed-in flags crossed in gratitude. Now this *other* Nell Taylor, probably about the same age, in the same grueling job as my great aunt, the same endlessness we all start with but she never came back. Innocence *and* experience. Which double door had I slipped through?

I'm told it means nothing, a shrug, a mere coincidence, a conflicting happenstance that clicks open and shut: one war, two Nell Taylors, two countries behind them, both of them ambulance drivers for the wounded and loss-whelmed. I can't help it: what if each had seen and spoken with her *other*, a kind of mirroring, each the other's secret self? Had they thought it wonderful and strange and funny, or a disturbing sign that they shared a name and a fearlessness?

Or right, of course they never met. Innocence is not ignorance, Blake wrote. And what of *experience*, the long coming after, graved in exhaustion and great care on the other side of those copper plates? I'm most haunted by that plaque's last phrase, the word "gift" set against the eternal present of noun turned verb turned dark-endless adjective, "sorrowing"—it keeps going. *The gift of her sorrowing parents*: imagine one of them writing that and showing it to the other.

The thing about Blake printing those twenty-seven copies we still have of his *Songs* is this: they changed through the years as he labored over one set, then another and another. He got better. It was never simple or rote; he never knew what would happen. The work crushed him and the world didn't give a good damn. Sometimes he had blue ink, not black, or mainly yellow pigment for his paint, his stock of green too low to matter much, more or less, this and that.

Don't dare pity him. The colors deepened, grew richer, layered, beyond luminous.

The Little Death of Self

The large word "I"
perhaps a flint shard
some toothless person used to scrape his
grisly meat.
　　—Gunnar Ekelof

Now I resemble a sort of god
Floating through the air in my soul-shift
Pure as a pane of ice. It's a gift.
　　—Sylvia Plath

You may not remember the *Hindenburg*. Or if you do, you may not remember it blowing up again and again by way of that marvelous television program, *The Twentieth Century*, hosted by Walter Cronkite every week, his show—through my childhood, at least—in its before-supper, on the air Sunday slot, key moments caught in black and white as he ran clips from the Great Depression, the Jazz Era, both World Wars. But it's the *Hindenburg* that stands out, most eccentric of flying machines, the giant German dirigible lumbering miraculously into view as Herbert Morrison, the self-assured young reporter from Chicago on the scene that day in New Jersey, 1937, narrated for radio this seeming apparition. Because all was not well. Famously, it simply—are these things ever simple?—caught fire in a matter of seconds, filling the screen with flames, coming apart at blurry bright angles, coming down. *O, the humanity!* the reporter even more famously cries out. You may remember that, the saddest of exclamations flashed urgent and broken in the air and, since then, repeated, parodied even, superimposed on all manner of fevered situations.

The real scene keeps coming, immediate and intact. One can see this particular disaster over and over on YouTube now. Push a button, fiddle with the keyboard to bring it back any time. I suppose—if your DNA carries the right techie gene—you could play it backward even, watch it come together again, its flame receding to nothing-at-all, the faces once more staring serenely out the small windows down to a world of onlookers thrilled by the spectacle.

When I was a kid, it was the instant tragedy that kicked in first, the high visuals of it, the thing flaming up, dropping down in shreds. But it's the sound of the commentary that stays with me, that voice-over, the sudden shift from alert, matter-of-fact reporter-guy to disbelief, to horror, to the sputter-unto-silence of the completely overwhelmed, to the purest cry imaginable in that lasting exclamation—*O, the humanity!* That's the personal take on this brief historical narrative. That remains its drama.

As I watch and listen to it now, it's how the reporter *recovers* that moves me. He's polite even in his frenzy. *Please, please, get out of the way* as he jockeys for a better view, or his repeated *oh ladies and gentlemen!* after his stunned no-way-to-describe-it. There's the riveting moment he must look away—*I'm sorry, honestly I can hardly breathe, I'm going to step inside where I cannot see it.* He does vanish then, probably for three or four minutes, though the audio we have now awkwardly patches it through for us as if no time has passed before he returns with a different voice, seemingly centered now, rearranged, to give context, reassure, do his job as card-carrying responsible grown-up who must make order out of such drastic disorder: the stats at hand now: how many aboard, how many saved and lost, and so on.

The reporter's whole rich reaction, the altered diction and emphasis start to finish, is a kind of EKG of tonal variation, his shifts fulfilling the second of Wallace Stevens' arch and most angelic requirements for any decent poem: *it must change.* And if this disaster were a poem, Tony Hoagland would call this its real story, defining that—as he has in an essay—as the emotional movement beneath the surface run of events. Note the *Hindenburg*'s terrible end: dirigible blows up and burns, X number are killed; what happens is clear enough and truly absorbing. Still, it's the personal voice that tracks *our* fate. We descend into the hell of his witnessing too, this speaker, this "I" who thus earns our belief. Through the young reporter we see and feel as he does. The interior drama is profoundly lyric; it includes us, brings us close even as the actual narrative *out there* shocks and distances. That this is, in part, a political act—the individual voice to be treasured in our age of insipid mass culture and group-think-alike—probably goes without saying. The point is that there's detail and progression, interior *story*, in a lyric poem. How we mess with both levels could be called *style*, I suppose. But the substance is clear: something matters beyond the bare-bones public facts, and that, too, must be told. Donald Hall's notion of a poem, his "inside person talking to inside person," rings true enough. It's the speaker we trust, however secret and solitary the voice that *comes to* via each poem's turn of image and idea.

But there's a noticeable shift from this approach, a growing wish in contemporary poetry to discredit or fracture, even rub out forever just such a speaker, a new impatience with genuinely *lived* experience as the source of poetry. Or it's a need to remain as hidden as possible. Or a desire for deeper play and outright accident, to e-invent, to *flarf*, cleverly collaging bits from the Web to leave behind the tired old real and potentially embarrassing—read: *sentimental*—self-as-speaker. Whatever the reasons, I hear and overhear this sometimes: *I want to kill the "I" in my poem*, as if that could move any mountain. And it's earnest, this wish, and somehow seductive though it seems a little like a Mobius strip, doesn't it? Or the serpent eating its own tail since the most convincing element in such an assertion lies at the very start and keeps sticking.

After all, who wants with such passion to *do in* that "I"? *I do I do I do*.

The fact is: poems aren't written by robots, and even if such a thing were arguable, those robots would be cleverly disguised as human beings. Lived experience does matter. *Someone* writes these things. Because poetry's long tradition is a full-body-press on that voice to make it personal. Can we ever get away from that? An expectation of intimacy comes through the direct use of *I*, the first-person pronoun, or it's implied through language, quirks of phrasing as revealing as bad penmanship acquired over years of proud effort. What many claim to be the first personal lyric in English, written in the late 1400s by an anonymous poet, goes this way:

> O Western wind, when wilt thou blow
> That the small rain down can rain?
> Christ, that my love were in my arms,
> And I in my bed again!

Christ! And you *hear* that outburst, that change as the piece moves from rather high diction, an invocation really, a plea, and frantic, for a warmer wind. *Christ,* he says to begin something more private and colloquial, the speaker squarely facing his own isolation. That this transition is preset but held off for a quiet second by the sweet, darkly strange single-stressed "small rain down can rain" might only appear if we X-rayed the poem and developed the film in the evil chemical rinse of our looking so closely. Note in such an X-ray how dramatically this lyric goes inward, how convincingly (exclamation point and all) it moves from that flash of the great world to an ordinary life, from the world's furious real weather to the experience of loss and serious desire. End of story.

But things never end in poems, particularly in lyrics. Here the deepest need—for love, for home, for things to have a bearable end—continues and rings true, not only through the words chosen but even in sentence structure, exclamation morphing into question, then all's emphatic again. As with the young reporter who freezes and unfreezes while the Hindenburg burns into history, we're allowed *in* through these changes—the human voice played off this syntax—even its painful pauses coming clear by way of line breaks and punctuation.

It's impossible, I think, to overestimate the importance of such a voice, how it carries authority partly because of its vulnerability, how it rises and falls and thus gets our attention. Because of it things *do* change, as Stevens advised. Even in the oldest poems, those considered epic—*Beowulf,* for instance—we're hit from the start with a speaker quite singular, a conduit for a tale

already ancient in the telling. *So.* I really mean the word "so."
Thus begins Seamus Heaney's translation with this surprisingly
informal one-word launch.

So. The Spear-Danes in days gone by
and the kings who ruled them had courage and greatness.
We have heard of those princes' heroic campaigns.

That this large *we* morphs so effortlessly to singular first per-
son by line 20 of this vast poem is significant: *I have never heard
before of a ship so well furbished.* From then on, that fiercely per-
sonal awe is a baseline sound, a crucial lyric intervention in the
drama allowing us to see vividly some fourteen centuries later.
Beowulf is, admittedly, full of fabulous exploits not the speaker's,
the voice functioning as recaller-in-chief of what's handed down.
But however story-bound this epic is for history's sake or simply
for bragging rights, the presence of an individual speaker gives
the poem an interior tension which stops time as is the lyric's in-
ward habit even as the epic's narrative energy is the real engine,
forcing the lively, bloody, very public accumulation forward.

When a poetic speaker focuses narrowly on his own experi-
ence, a deeper stain enters the mix. Example: a lyric ancestor
to "O Western Wind" surely, from roughly the same time as *Be-
owulf*, a lament by a *scop*—a medieval poet—who's been over-
shadowed by another singer and cruelly thrown out of patron-
age, undone like so many others, including those destroyed by
someone called Eormanric and his "wolfish mind." And "many
a warrior sat expecting woe," he first tells us, spreading the bad
news around, "in his soul, it grows dark." But soon this speaker
is as direct as Job about his suffering.

This is my self I wish to say—
that for a time I was the gleeman of the Heodenings . . .
Deor was my name. . . .
I had for many winters a good employment, a gracious lord,
until now Heorrenda, a song-skilled man,
received the land-rights that to me the protector of earls had
    given before.
As that passed away, so may this.

And what started as a piece that included others winnows down to one stricken speaker obsessed with his own troubles. When does the personal become too much? The very first lyrics, we're told, were laments, songs broken and loud above graves or next to funeral pyres before anything was written down or set to memory. But the grief was for someone else. Here, this poor scop's pity is self-pity, to comfort himself that as others' trials have "passed away, so may this." When my friend and Purdue colleague, Mary Neipokuj, a historical linguist, showed me this poem, we agreed half-jokingly that it might well be the first honest-to-god *whine* in English.

I want to kill the "I" in my poem. Is this in answer, then, to the grand tradition of what we called when I was growing up *just feeling sorry for yourself,* a state of mind before which someone, some wise-ass friend no doubt, would have plenty to say, that iconic single-stressed bit of advice, for starters: get a grip!

But this particular shadow on the lyric impulse does haunt me, especially when I think of certain readings I've attended, the self-absorbed speaker in the poems too prominent, those evenings on-again, off-again so hard to sit through, flush with detail pointlessly revealing—however accurate the complaint about family or work or sex—moments that give confessional poetry a bad name, one checkpoint—armed or not—away from pure gossip. In that light, it's easy to concede. Kill the *I?* Okay, so maybe there are reasons. But not to censor entire swatches of subject matter, instead to adjust the lens, widen it to a flash that begins exactly at the point self-involvement fades or at least can morph to something far more mysterious, and interesting.

In any case, the whole idea grows complex, beyond what I first thought largely a next generation's rebellion against that confessional mode, itself a revolt in the '60s and '70s to free poetry from the academic, the heavy-handed, from an indifference to ordinary life. In fact, if you count poor Deor's lament for self and circumstance, these *kill-the-I* warriors have a much longer paper trail and word-hoard to battle, back to the eighth century at least.

To battle, or absorb. There are ways.

Because there *have been ways*: shrewd or blundering, serious or comic, ways found by accident or design, predictable ways or no-one-in-her-right-mind-could-imagine, pretty much impossible ways to enter a poem and keep it going. That must be the heart of this anxiety about "killing the I," how to find footing as the maker of the poem without seeming to exactly, to let thought and experience rise from a personal grounding, up the most interior passages of the body until there's a voice—credible, human, as transparent as possible—that might be a conduit. Finding *that* is the miracle that makes any poem about-to-happen.

About-to-happen. But to manage that, the reverse comes crucial too: that something *stop* happening for once, right there at the start of the making. Do we really write poems to *find* ourselves, as so often is promised? The sweet thing goes deeper: to lose the self, to make room for something else.

First such quiet to call down, a pure selflessness, something else I remember from that long-lost television screen too, an emptiness when Walter Cronkite stopped talking and the reporter was yet to speak. It seemed simple enough, the hand-held camera steady a moment: a square of afternoon sky there, its vast, grainy nothing-at-all before the doomed *Hindenburg* drifted into view. And then, the other great quieting—*I'm going to step inside where I cannot see it*—as the young reporter finds he *must* look away to see clearly, to see anything at all.

That drift then, not much perhaps, just something to wait through. But the strongest poetry I know keeps company with such an emptiness, no matter how privately disastrous and compelling the subject, the first-person position as muted as it is revealing. Evidence: an uncharacteristically short poem by Lucia Perillo, a writer who usually takes on the dramatic lyric full force, with dense, often wry, story-advancing detail. Here in the title poem of her early collection *The Body Mutinies*, the moment is grave and brief, opened with much grace and tact just as a life fully changes for the worst, though how bad it could be we—seeing as the speaker does—can't know yet. What's clear is how common this exchange must be: the speaker gets very bad news from her doctor. But the stunned silence involved—there's that drift again—is immense. Here are its full fourteen lines.

When the doctor runs out of words and still
I won't leave, he latches my shoulder and
steers me out doors. Where I see his blurred hand,
through the milk glass, flapping goodbye like a sail
(& me not griefstruck yet but still amazed: how
words and names—medicine's blunt instruments—
undid me. And the seconds, those half seconds
it took for him to say those words.) For now,
I'll just stand in the courtyard, watching bodies
struggle in then out of one lean shadow
a tall fir lays across the wet flagstones,
before the sun clears the valance of gray trees
and finds the surgical-supply shop window
and makes the dusty bedpans glint like coins.

If a backstory is needed here—Perillo herself hit with multiple sclerosis decades ago—so be it. But this rides powerfully without that, like a good ekphrastic poem carries on quite well, pretty much without the painting that inspired it directly at hand. What's remarkable about this first-person voice is how modest it is, just a lens such sights past through in a charged situation, confined pretty much to stage directions: "I won't leave . . . I see . . . I'll just stand in the courtyard" so we have a place to witness *from*, both physically and emotionally. The exception is signaled by the secret-making parentheses surrounding more interior news—"& me not griefstruck yet" or "how medicine's blunt instruments—undid me." But a more lasting loss suggests itself as the speaker recounts in slow, beautiful increments a catalogue of the small things available in such a moment, the world beyond the speaker changing, still ordinary but now darkly radiant with meaning because all at once we're on the farther side of that thick curtain dividing *before* from *after*: first the doctor's "blurred hand" there, behind the milky door, then those outside who "struggle" through the "one lean shadow" cast by a towering fir tree. And most immoveable and heart-chilling of all, that surgical supply store, its window filled with "dusty bedpans" glinting "like coins."

The last five lines carry these images straight. We forget, in the pleasure and pain of Perillo's detail, that it's the speaker of the poem seeing all this in her new state as *marked person*. We forget because it's no longer only her story. It's been released to us through the clarity and quiet selflessness of the telling. What started in response to the most personal of assaults has ended in wonder. It's passed to a "woe, world-sorrow" as another poet, Gerard Manley Hopkins, called such a thing.

How poets get larger, how they can use the first person more as catapult than simply as an exhaustive limiting zoom lens on their life-so-far; is that part of the issue here? What if there are extremes of mind so interior and unfathomable that they must intrude, taking over every bit of breathing space in the poem?

Hopkins' "world-sorrow" is not exactly where he begins, I think. A writer of great emotional extremes, this late-nineteenth-century British poet seems someone—and I've worried this thought before—who when he sat down to write, must have jacked himself up or down to extraordinary levels of mind and heart not usually found between breakfast and supper in a normal life. His poems, after all, track a flood of realization so over-brimming, either in ecstasy or cast to the darkest depths. Could anyone live full-time like that and stay sane?

All poets have favorite psychic spots, places of comfort and tension enough to dare the work on. We develop habits to ensure such states of being, not all of them so healthy. But finding a recognizable *private* speaker must have been a tricky business for Hopkins, locked as he was in a kind of professional offing of the self through his vocation as a Jesuit priest, thus his pledge of allegiance *not* to personal expression (and certainly not fame). Poems—if they be written at all—had to honor divine glory. So it can't be surprising that when the "I" appears in Hopkins' poems, it often suggests the generic one-who-prays, more a small votive candle burning somewhere in the corner of a church rather than a personal presence with all the messy parapher-nalia of a lived life in tow. In addition, there's this: reading his poems often means waiting for the some telltale mention of the godhead, some otherworldly shoe to drop hard.

It's staggering, given the Jesuit's gag order, how flushed through with personal verve Hopkins' poems are anyway. Who else but *this* particular poet could buckle down to prayer by nailing his gratitude for the curious "dappled" beauty of summer, for its "skies of couple-colour as a brinded cow" or

Fresh-firecoal chestnut-falls; finches' wings;
Landscape plotted and pieced—fold, fallow, and plough;
And all trades, their gear and tackle and trim.
All things counter, original, spare, strange;
Whatever is fickle, freckled (who knows how?)
With swift, slow; sweet, sour; adazzle, dim. . . .

So goes a large part of his well-known "Pied Beauty" with its riot of image and adjective, the natural world caught by one very alert, specific-heat-seeking speaker. In a letter to his friend Robert Bridges, Hopkins' ideal for a poem—or any work of art—was telling. Its beauty, he claimed, depended on the artist bringing out "all the complex individuality of the subject" which, in effect, brings out "the individuality of the artist." Meaning: what is said defines who's saying it, or loosely put in a borrowed way: *I see by my outfit.* So even without a speaker owning up through a first-person pronoun, it's obvious who's talking, singing, or completely beside himself. That ideal weighed on Hopkins, pointing back always to the solitary one-who-writes. "Every poet," he wrote to Bridges in 1878, "must be original and originality the condition of poetic genius; so that each poet is like a species in nature and cannot recur."

Such a high expectation gets Hopkins in trouble though. Even Bridges took him to task for his "oddness," his "affectation," his "obscurity." In our own last century, the cranky, most insightful critic Paul Fussell, for one, impatiently dismissed this poet from the "history of English versification," relegating him instead to the "history of personal British eccentricity," high praise in my book though apparently not in Fussell's though he got the "eccentric" part right. Hopkins' voice stands thoroughly soaked in image and turns of diction so surprising, so downright quirky that we know instantly, with deep joy (fulfilling, by the way, Stevens first rule for poetry: *it must give pleasure*), that we're in the presence of a mind and method powerful and unique. In his so-called "dark sonnets" too, where a seemingly personal "I" does take charge, it's what Fussell deems so wrong—an emotionally charged, overstressed natural speech—that brilliantly sticks. "I wake," the poet begins #44, the well-loved, most despondent of these pieces, "and feel the fall of dark, not day." From there it only grows bleaker, to fill out what that terrible "selfyeast" feels like.

I am gall, I am heartburn. God's most deep decree
Bitter would have me taste: my taste was me.
Bones built in me, fleshed filled, blood brimmed the curse.

Are the speaker's self-railings here all that removed from Deor's private rants? Or from an embarrassing night of bad confessional poetry heard last month or last year?

Yes! Because beyond his rich language and image, his finely tuned ear, the great difference lies in Hopkins' coming straight off his vows: these late and haunted sonnets, like his ecstatic work, are cast as prayer. They're wired up to go *someplace else*, to escape beyond complaint and self-scrutiny through whatever small window of hope for forgiveness Hopkins gives them, however locked the poems are in their anguish-ridden weight and counterweight. Finally they're directed outward, in a very long reach.

I say that as an agnostic who, as a child, was right there at Mass, in wholehearted belief. A few years ago though, driving the three hours home from Chicago, my husband and I tuned in NPR and heard the composer John Corrigliano interviewed, holding forth on the historical shift in music over the last two centuries. *Before Wagner* and *After Wagner* is how he set that line. What he meant, he said, was simple: *Before*—composers were writing *to* God. *After*—they've been writing *as* God.

So did lightning strike our SONY speaker in that car? Was the radio itself forever after a charred, smoking tangle of wires and circuits?

Absolutely. Cross my heart.

It's an idea almost too dangerous to consider, although to be fair, Corrigliano's concern was largely with composers blithely forsaking melody, which must be the musical equivalent to a clear narrative line. He worried about the audience left behind in the fast-approaching atonal chaos, post-Wagner. But regarding poetic voice, what does speaking "as god" really mean? Speaking *to* God implies a human being let loose on the page, after all, flawed, vulnerable. We recognize that common lyric stance; we identify with it, even as nonbelievers. But to speak *as* God? The nerve involved, the high-flying oxygen deprivation . . . . Of course, fiction writers who practice full-fledged omniscience in their narration might not feel this an amazing turn at all. Is it simply, then, a matter of shifting to third person and calling it quits?

"I heard a fly buzz when I died," Emily Dickinson begins what must be the most stellar of her greatest hits. But tweak that to a more all-knowing stance—"*She* heard a fly buzz when *she* died"—and the line goes flat on the heart monitor. Or consider Robert Frost, Dickinson's compatriot decades later in the same New England, his very personal speaker so fully exhausted after days of apple picking one fall, how heightened moments in that poem gain or lose by our ditching his "*I* keep hearing from the cellar bin / the rumbling sound of load on load of apples / coming in" for third person's more distant god-like perspective. Make the change. Check it out.

> And *one* keeps hearing from the cellar bin
> the rumbling sound of load on load of apples
> coming in. For *one* can have too much
> of apple picking. *One* gets overtired
> of the great harvest *one* oneself desires.

Gone: intensity. Gone: every edgy thing you might have loved about this poem. The new distance in the voice would be comic if it weren't so decidedly *ho-hum.* The temperature just dropped about fifty degrees.

This substitution is cheap, I know, if not actively really really stupid. If Frost had written this *as God*, who knows what treasure he might have unearthed here? Because he *does* manage a third-person lockdown and its deliberate weight, sometimes in pieces fully narrative—his "Out, Out" for instance—or in briefer ones, near-aphorisms as "Design" or "Fire and Ice" though in such pieces he often narrowly keeps that godlike stance out of it, startling us with a sudden entry of an "I" who sadly agrees or turns the subject inside-out. In "After Apple-Picking," if fully buying into this trade of first person for third, surely he would have lost the sense of human failure, and that humility, a *not-knowing* much at all finally—how things work or never work—in short, the lyric poignancy you just can't shake. In the poem he left us, Frost examines such exhaustion—physical, spiritual—without melodrama, ending in the lowest key:

> Were he not gone, the woodchuck would say
> whether it's like his long sleep, as I describe
> its coming on, or just some human sleep.

As I describe its coming on. The speaker owning up again is crucial, taking us back in a swift half second over the whole dire business, giving reason—or release—for and to something immeasurably darker waiting past the poem's end, a slow, awful ticking there. And—this is the worst thing—eventually we'll all hear it.

That imagined sound, so much like the tick tick tick of Dickinson's infamous and unholy fly. To reconsider that poem in Corrigliano's light is to see she's the one neck and neck with Richard Wagner, pretty much her contemporary anyway. But the notion of Dickinson talking *as* God? She was, in fact, deep in that celestial upgrade and fast approaching the zone where divine lightning might strike after all. That fly in her poem, then—check. The deathbed room itself—check. The "Stillness" there—check. Those "Eyes around" . . . "And Breaths" as the dying speaker fades and her "Keepsakes" willed away. "What portion of me be / Assignable" she tells us in a sudden wry aside before recalling once more, no,

> it was
> There interposed a Fly—
>
> With Blue—uncertain stumbling Buzz—
> Between the light—and me—
> And then the Windows failed—and then
> I could not see to see—

Can you hear how impossibly modern that sounds? That "Blue—uncertain stumbling Buzz"? Modern *and* yes, godlike, I have to say. Because her use of that first person is most curious. Though still seemingly personal in the lyric's great tradition, Dickinson is, in fact, throwing her voice. Far more than one life is ending. And really, who is saying this? Plain fact: among her many admittedly bad poems that take on the classic sentimentality of nineteenth-century magazine verse (which this poet read avidly), Dickinson's best pieces have this peculiar genius about them, set some place beyond mortal time, seen dry-eyed in an eerie state of almost nonbeing. "I heard a Fly buzz—when I died—" she says. Past tense. We are *so* afterlife here—aren't we?—though perhaps that wasn't as odd as it might seem given her century's anxiety about burying people too soon, deathbed medical observation being what it was or wasn't, so many documented cases where the apparent dead came alive in the casket, even under the sod. (So many, actually, that some insisted on a so-called "premature burial device," most commonly a rope attached to their wrists when the time came, its length snaking up above ground to a bell which could ring out if they did *come to* after the mourners went home.) In any case, Dickinson's cool, near-magical eye in the poem looks down or vastly across by way of its immediate narrative detail: those *windows*, that *buzz*. Of course, there's the superb phrase: "and then / I could not see to see—" How that's said nails a personal vision meticulously disembodied, already shifting godlike. Her distant *unself*-concern nevertheless feels quite close. Which is to say this could be *our* end of life, *our* death signaled in that fly's dark stutter between eye and window.

Brigit Kelly and I have for years talked about what we call "the big voice," a cast of mind that assumes power without hesitation, the omniscient ring it has, how much pure nerve it takes to hold forth like that, an approach largely male in the past but now increasingly an equal-opportunity fix in American poetry. However trademark small and quiet her poems, set in opposition and equal to Whitman's loud expanse, Dickinson can carry off this "big voice" and, in that, she foreshadow decades in advance Wallace Stevens' last rule for poems—*it must be abstract*—even given the private, unsettling way such a voice comes across, first person or not. "Abstract" here, I'm taking to mean, suggests a turn bigger than self, than the self's concerns. We're beyond a *lived* life with this particular "I" of Dickinson's since—duh!—the speaker didn't die but instead—surprise—*has written this poem!* Its "I" participates in both worlds, as real as it is deeply imagined. And so is scary. Is steely. Is elastic. Is thrilling. Is big unto bigger.

And maybe it's viral. Maybe you can catch it, this not quite killing the "I," instead letting it morph, go strange—half hard-lived experience behind it, half dream—as you hover in those vacant pre-*Hindenburg* disaster moments where a poem's *about to happen*. And then it does, unfolding itself as various drafts come and go. Here's the word from John Keats on this: his well-known theory of "negative capability" where a poet must be "capable of being in uncertainties, Mysteries, doubts, without any irritable reaching after fact and reason." Which is to say: *it's not yours to finish.*

But viruses travel by touch, by air, by blood. Or the literary kind by such sure and gradual osmosis of affection that it seems a sudden afterthought that they've burrowed into us, poems written long before we were even a spot of DNA to be thus marked—or tainted—forever. That there's a straight line from Dickinson to Sylvia Plath must be tattooed on someone's right arm by now, someone about to earn tenure for it and a small jump in pay. Both poets are drawn to large assertions, making claims right and left; both share a fevered interiority that starves the poem on one hand and fills it to brimming on the other. So it's tempting to say that Plath, like Dickinson, is also "post-Wagnerian"—talking *as* God—with her fierce overview, her distant sound, lines like:

> The womb
> Rattles its pod, the moon
> Discharges itself from the tree with nowhere to go.

or

> Love is a shadow.
> How you lie and cry after it.

or

> This is the light of the mind, cold and planetary.

That this poet delivers from such heights, most commonly *abstracting* her legendary pain and discontent through this mix of image and statement, is something Dickinson managed a century earlier, but Plath takes it farther, following Aristotle's #1 requirement for poetic intelligence: a rage not for order or beauty but for metaphor. Plath defines even the self largely by metaphor, the more unnerving and accurate the better. She builds her poems with it, asking, as William Carlos Williams did: *what thing is shaped as this thing is shaped?* Poets *mean* through such unlikely welding, and even Keats weighed in on the subject, dismissing first what he called "the Wordsworthian or egotistical sublime" for something weirder, more slippery, having to do with poetic voice and its absolute dependence on metaphor. A poet, he wrote to a friend,

> is the most unpoetical of anything in existence; because he has no Identity—continually . . . filling some other body—the Sun, the sea, the Sea, and Men and Women who have about them an unchangeable attribute.

Continually . . . filling some other body. To define through images beyond the self makes an urgent metaphorical link between worlds: don't we imagine it's godlike to do that? "Only connect," Forster passionately advised. To X-ray everything so those ghostly points of similarity startle and shine in the most shadowy moment.

Practically any poem of Plath's would show off this dazzling addiction to metaphor. One of the smaller pieces in *Ariel,* her "Poppies in October," is an odd choice, I suppose, since certain elements seem cast in the *before Wagner* mold—talking *to* god— the flawed speaker undone by her realizations, their awful weight pressing down to trigger the final inward-breaking outburst that mirrors the despair in our oldest true lyric, "O Western Wind," its speaker's *Christ* in exclamation, then on to his sad *oh-would-that-everything-were-different.* But Plath clearly starts *in-medias-res,* by way of comparison and argument—"Even the sun-clouds this morning cannot. . . ." So right off, it's the terrible middle of something and this stately claiming voice, its perfect right to hold forth. What follows is her "Poppies in October," all twelve

lines of it done up in their stripped-down tercets, most unstable
of stanza forms.

> Even the sun-clouds this morning cannot manage such
>   skirts.
> Nor the woman in the ambulance
> Whose red heart blooms through her coat so astound-
>   ingly—
>
> A gift, a love gift
> Utterly unasked for
> By a sky
>
> Palely and flamily
> Igniting its carbon monoxides, by eyes
> Dulled to a halt under bowlers.
>
> Oh my God, what am I
> That these late mouths should cry open
> In a forest of frost, in a dawn of cornflowers.

A poem made of three sentences, the first end-stopped so ear-
ly and seemingly partial that it appears to be an announcement,
a dramatic flourish to signal a most emphatic start. As she goes
on, Plath reasons by analogy, as is her habit, and by color here,
honoring a full canvas and connecting what bloody dots she can.
Her moves start high (those "sun-clouds"), drop to the ground-
level poppies by way of straight-out metaphor ("such skirts")
through the grief-rimmed red shock of a medical emergency,
slipping coolly into commentary ("a gift, a love gift")—love-red,
it's clear—up again to sky, its poisons particular now, dangerous
("carbon monoxides") which are pale and could easily ignite
flame-red, and do, back to earth then, to well-dressed automa-
tons right out of Eliot's *Wasteland* who seem to be walking, who
definitely wear bowler hats, whose "eyes" are "dulled to a halt"
under them. Nothing and no one can witness or "manage" or
bear these poppies as the speaker can, or is forced to.

One might get dizzy, given a flow chart like this. The poet's
all over the place. But it's Plath's smart line breaks that slow the
gyrations, deliver them with distilled, quiet deliberation; not

hesitation, such pauses, the speaker too sure of herself, too *god-like* for that. Of course, it's that ambulance that takes us so deeply inside pure horror, past steel doors no doubt just slammed shut, into the body itself where the "red heart blooms" out "so astoundingly" that the most ordinary coat fills up; it's bloody, as red as the poppies that incited this poem, that initial stanza breaking off into the next by the urgent dash that Dickinson loved first and obsessively.

Four simple tercets maybe, but spookily sonnet-like if by *sonnet* one means a major turn in the poem's most serious business, a shift in voice at its end. So far nothing is carried forward by a first-person speaker; no "I" has directly owned up to seeing or imagining the ambulance, the sky, the poppies that clearly hypnotize and are the source of everything here. These images float on the page apparently by divine right and reportage: *they are they are they are* for us to notice, simple riveting facts served up all-knowingly from a godlike height.

But the speaker, of course, stains and skews such facts in the telling. A personal juice is nevertheless here in how things are described. What else but a voice set in motion by Plath could come up with blood that nevertheless *blooms* thrillingly through a coat, or with toxic threatening air to breathe that seems for a moment almost festive. Still, in the final three lines, an honest, full-blown "I" breaks through to shatter the brief silence of the stanza break, to rear up under the tonnage of all that comes before with an even darker charge:

> Oh my God, what am I
> That these late mouths should cry open.

We hear that, half question, half exclamation about self and world so pure and terrible, so tied to actual image—*who am I, alone condemned to see such things?*—the poppies now simplified horribly to "mouths" and such amplified red anguish that only one witness can hear and see, then dare put down these words.

One witness. Get that? *One.* That's the lyric, the great convincing single heartbeat in poems. And, as such, *our* conduit too. We see through those eyes. That speaker gives us a place *to be* in the poem. Stevens, agreeing with Keats, wrote this: "Poetry is not personal." But he also insisted, almost like Keats, that "a poet confers his identity on the reader." He called it "a transference." Then he added this in his notebook: "Poets acquire humanity." *Acquire.* As if that's viral too, a good virus, a slow welling up, that humanity. It takes a long time.

In the first poem of his first book, Frost wrote simply: *you come too*, a wish that seems an afterthought except that he said it again in that poem so we could almost call it a refrain. Which is to say, a human voice and a phrase that includes the sorry likes of us most emphatically, still, these years and years later.

One last thought about this, or maybe just an image.

Not too long ago, I was unaccountably privileged, allowed to descend into the underworld twelve hours each week, attending the so-called *cadaver lab* in Indiana University's medical school on my campus at Purdue, suiting up in blue scrubs and rubber gloves each Monday, Wednesday, and Friday with sixteen first-year medical students, each armed with scalpel, forceps, hemostat, and whatever raw, rare courage they could muster.

Over those months we cut and peered into the most private regions of the body—four bodies, two men, two women, all over seventy, the press of years upon them—down to the most hidden spinal cord and kidney, cervix and prostate, furious cross-hatching of arteries and nerves, dizzy swirl of colon, the mismatched unidentical lungs we held in our hands to feel the air, still inside. And their hands, the etching in the thick-skinned palms we traced, then peeled back to bone and muscle so multiple, in its strings and layers. But always the heads were secret, kept hidden from us. Shrouded in thick soaked towels most of the term, they sank back on the tables as we probed and stripped tissue and fat and bone from clavicle to the most distant provinces of the lower limbs. But who were these people? Finally, late November, all was dissected, except the head. Then we unwrapped them. For the first time, after weeks and weeks, we were eye to eye.

Those heads, so beautiful I could hardly breathe. Such heart-stopping particularity, charcoal line of cheekbone and lip, bridge of nose, forehead, intricate spiral of ear. Before, all had been private enough, places we had no right to: groin and hand, abdomen and breast. But how little that meant now, before such faces looming up: *exactly who they were and no one else.* Only now were they human, each fully different than the others, individuals with specific lives, childhoods somewhere back there frozen in the brain, memories of afternoons, years of sleep and dream in those faces, hard work, sorrow, deceit, remorse, joy, pride, indifference, rage. But something else too: they were finally the dead; they were everyone who had ever lived.

Oh the humanity, that young reporter cried out and keeps crying, stepping away to blank it all out for a moment, to quiet himself to continue, the film cataloged for history, played on a computer now by anyone, anytime. Those cadavers: I can't pretend they stared at us; three of them seemed to be sleeping. The fourth, the oldest, looked out of her watery blue eyes at nothing, and no one.

It's puzzling; it contradicts. Maybe the individual face *is* the most public part of the body, the way it mirrors back whatever it sees, as Keats says the poet must absorb, and thus lose himself to open at all. Still, each face is *what it is,* private, unique as any turn of voice in a poem must be, because that *is* the poem, in whatever edgy way it takes shape.

Do you believe such a voice? Can you hear it? All meaning comes through that.

Works Cited or Consulted

Accardo, Pasquale. *Diagnosis and Detection: the Medical Iconography of Sherlock Holmes*. Rutherford, NJ: Fairleigh Dickinson University Press, 1987.

Aristotle. *The Physics*. Translated by Philip Wicksteed and Francis Cornford. Cambridge, MA: Harvard University Press, 1957.

Abbot, Louise. "Remembering Flannery." *Flannery O'Connor Bulletin* 23 (1994–1995).

Ackroyd, Peter. *Blake*. New York: Knopf, 1996.

Andrews, Tom. *The Collected Poems of Tom Andrews*. Oberlin, OH: Oberlin College Press, 2002.

Augustine. *Confessions*. Translated and edited by Philip Burton. New York: Knopf, 2001.

Beethoven, Ludwig van. *Piano Concerto #5, op. 73*. Glenn Gould with the Toronto Symphony Orchestra. http://www.youtube.com/watch?v=4 19h93TiCFg&feature=related

Bell, Joseph. "A Note on Sherlock Holmes," from *A Study in Scarlet*. London: Ward, Lock, 1893.

Bently, G. E. Jr. *Blake Records*. Oxford: Clarendon Press, 1969.

Bently, G. E. Jr. *Blake Records Supplement*. Oxford: Clarendon Press, 1988.

Berger, John. *The Sense of Sight*. New York: Pantheon Books, 1985.

Berryman, John. *77 Dream Songs*. New York: Farrar, Straus & Giroux, 1964.

Berryman, John. Interview with Peter Stitt, *Paris Review*, Winter 1972.

Bindman, David. *Blake as an Artist*. Oxford: Phaidon and Dutton, 1977.

Binnick, Robert. *Time and the Verb: A Guide to Tense and Aspect*. New York: Oxford University Press, 1991.

Bishop, Elizabeth. *The Complete Poems*. New York: Farrar, Straus & Giroux, 1983.

Bishop, Elizabeth. "Flannery O'Connor, 1925–1964." *New York Review of Books*, Oct. 8, 1964.

Bishop, Elizabeth. *Geography III*. New York: Farrar, Straus & Giroux, 1976.

Bishop, Elizabeth. "Interior with Extension Cord," in *Exchanging Hats*, edited by William Benton. ([undated], watercolor, gouache, and ink, 6 1/8 by 6 1/8 inches. Collection of Loren MacIver, 43.) New York: Farrar, Straus & Giroux, 1996.

Bishop, Elizabeth. *Letters to Flannery O'Connor (Box 1, Folder 9, the Sally Fitzgerald papers), Rose Manuscript, Archives & Rare Book Library*, Emory University, Atlanta, GA.

Bishop, Elizabeth. *One Art*. Edited by Robert Giroux. New York: Farrar, Straus & Giroux 1994.

Bishop, Elizabeth, and Robert Lowell. *Words in Air: The Complete Correspondence of Elizabeth Bishop and Robert Lowell*. Edited by Thomas Travisano and Saskia Hamilton. New York: Farrar, Straus & Giroux, 2008. (WIA)

Blake, William. *Complete Writings*. Edited by Geoffrey Keynes, London: Oxford University Press, 1971.

Blake, William. *The Letters of William Blake*. Edited by Geoffrey Keynes. Oxford: Clarendon Press, 1980.

Blake, William. *The Note-Book of William Blake*. Edited by Geoffrey Keynes, New York: Cooper Square Publishing, 1970.

Blake, William. *Songs of Innocence and Experience*. Edited by Robert Essick. San Marino, CA: Huntington Library, 2008.

Blake, William. *Songs of Innocence and Experience*. Edited by Andrew Lincoln. Vol. 2 of *Blake's Illuminated Books*. Princeton, NJ: Princeton University Press, 1991.

Bleich, Alan Ralph. *The Story of X-Rays*, New York: Dover, 1960.

Boland, Eavan, trans. *After Every War: Twentieth-Century Woman Poets*. Princeton NJ: Princeton University Press, 2004.

Boland, Eavan. *In a Time of Violence*. New York: Norton, 1994.

Bolcom, William. Liner notes, *Songs of Innocence and Experience*. Naxos, American Classics Series, 2004.

Bybee, Joan, Revere Perkins, and William Pagliuca. *The Evolution of Grammar: Tense, Aspect, and Modality in the Languages of the World*. Chicago: University of Chicago Press, 1994.

Campell, Rev. Paul E., and Sister Mary Donatus MacNickle. *Voyages in English*. Chicago: Loyola University Press, 1951.

Cooper, Astley. *Surgical Lectures*. London: Cox and Son (et al.), 1818.

Da Vinci, Leonardo. *The Notebooks of Leonardo da Vinci*. Edited and translated by Edward MacCurdy, New York: Braziller, 1954.

Dickinson, Emily. *The Complete Poems of Emily Dickinson*. Edited by Thomas H. Johnson. Boston: Little Brown, 1970.

Doyle, Arthur Conan. A flip book of self-portraits. Archives, Surgeons' Hall Museum, Edinburgh, Scotland, UK.

Doyle, Arthur Conan. *A Study in Scarlet.* Chicago: Donohue, Henneberry and Co, 1895.

Draaisma, Douwe. *Metaphors of Memory: A History of Ideas about the Mind.* Cambridge: Cambridge University Press, 2000.

Eberhardt, Scott, and Anderson, David. "How Airplanes Work: A Physical Description of Lift." *Aviation,* February 1999.

Edgerton, Samuel. *The Renaissance Rediscovery of Linear Perspective.* New York: Basic Books, 1975.

Edson, Russell. "The Prose Poem in America." *Parnassus* 5, no. 1 (1976).

Edwards, Betty. *Drawing on the Artist Within.* New York: Simon and Schuster, 1986.

Edwards, Betty. *Drawing on the Right Side of the Brain,* Los Angeles, CA: Tarcher, 1989.

Ekelof, Gunnar. *Friends, You Drank Some Darkness: Three Swedish Poets, Harry Martinson, Gunnar Ekelof and Tomas Transtromer.* Edited and translated by Robert Bly. St. Paul, MN: Seventies Press, 1972.

Eliot, T. S. *The Complete Poems,* New York: Harcourt, Brace & World, 1962.

Eliot, T. S. "Silence." In *Eliot's Early Years,* edited by Gordon, Lyndall. New York: Farrar, Strass & Giroux, 1977.

Emerson, Ralph Waldo. *Selected Essays, Lectures and Poems.* Edited by Robert Spiller. New York: Washington Square Press, 1965.

Freud, Sigmund. *Collected Papers.* Translated by Joan Riviere. London: Hograth Press, 1950.

Frost, Robert. *The Poetry of Robert Frost.* Edited by Edward Connery Lathem. New York: Holt, Rinehart and Winston, 1969.

Frost, Robert. *The Selected Prose of Robert Frost.* Edited by Hyde Cox and Edward Connery Lathem. New York: Random House, 1979.

Fussell, Paul. *Poetic Meter and Poetic Form.* New York: Random House, 1965.

Gerrberg, Mort. *Cartooning: The Art and the Business.* New York: William Morrow, 1989.

Gimlette, John D. *Malay Poisons and Charm Cures.* London: J. and A. Churchille, 1929.

Ginsberg, Allen, *Deliberate Prose: Selected Essays 1952–1995.* Edited by Bill Morgan. New York: Harper Collins, 2000.

Gluck, Louise. *The Triumph of Achilles.* New York: Ecco, 1985.

Goldstein, Nathan. *The Art of Responsive Drawing.* Englewood Cliffs, NJ: Prentice-Hall, 1973.

Gooch, Brad. *Flannery: A Life of Flannery O'Connor.* NY: Little Brown, 2009. (FOC)

Gregory, Richard L. *Eye and Brain.* New York: McGraw-Hill, 1981.

Gross, Harvey. *Sound and Form in Modern Poetry*. Ann Arbor: University of Michigan Press, 1968.

Halliday, Mark. "Chinese Leftovers." *Denver Quarterly*, Summer 1988.

Hass, Robert. *Twentieth Century Pleasures: Prose on Poetry*. New York: Ecco, 1984.

Hayden, Robert. *Collected Poems*. New York: Liveright, 1985.

Heaney, Seamus. *Selected Poems, 1966–1996*. New York: Farrar, Straus & Giroux, 1998.

Hecht, Anthony. *Collected Earlier Poems*. New York: Knopf, 1990.

Hoagland, Tony. *Real Sofistikashun*. St. Paul, MN: Graywolf Press, 2006.

Hopkins, Gerard Manley. *The Prose and Poems of Gerard Manley Hopkins*. New York: Penguin, 1986.

Hunter, John. *Letters from the Past: From John Hunter to Edward Jenner, 1775*. Edited by E. H. Cornelius and A. J. H. Rains. London: Royal College of Surgeons, 1976,

Jakab, Peter L. *Visions of a Flying Machine*. Washington, DC: Smithsonian Institution Press, 1990.

Jensen, Laura. *Shelter*. Port Townsend, WA: Dragon Gate, 1985.

Kafka, Francis. *Linoleum Block Printing*. New York: Dover, 1955.

Kamien, Roger. *Understanding Music: An Appreciation*. Boston: McGraw-Hill, 2000.

Keats, John. *Complete Poetry and Selected Prose of John Keats*. Edited by Harold Briggs. New York: Random House, 1951.

Keats, John. *John Keats's Anatomical and Physiological Note Book*. Edited by Maurice Forman. Oxford: Oxford University Press, 1934.

Keats, John. *The Keats Circle: Letters and Papers, 1816–1878*. Edited by Hyder Edward Rollins. Cambridge, MA: Harvard University Press, 1948.

Keats, John. *The Letters of John Keats*. Edited by Maurice Buxton Forman. Oxford, UK: Oxford University Press, 1931.

Keel, Jeffery. "Inner Visions," *Vegetarian Times*, March 2001.

Kelly, Brigit Pegeen. *Song*. Brockport, NY: BOA Editions, 1995.

Kenyon, Jane. *The Book of Quiet Hours*. St. Paul, MN: Graywolf Press, 1986.

King, Lester. *Medical Thinking: An Historical Preface*. Princeton, NJ: Princeton University Press, 1982.

La Barre, Weston. "Anthropological Perspectives on Hallucinations and Hallucinogens," *Hallucinations: Behavior, Experience, and Theory*. New York: John Wiley and Sons, 1975.

Larkin, Philip. *Required Writing*. Ann Arbor: University of Michigan Press, 1999.

Lee, Li-Young. *Rose*. Brockport, NY: BOA Editions, 1986.

Levy-Bruhl, Lucien. *The Notebooks on Primitive Mentality*. Oxford: Basil Blackwell, 1975.

Lockwood, Lewis. *Beethoven: The Music and the Life*. New York: Norton, 2003.

Lowell, Robert. *Life Studies*. New York: Farrar, Straus & Giroux, 1976.

MacNeice, Louis. *The Collected Poems*. London: Faber and Faber, 1966.

Monteiro, George. *Conversations with Elizabeth Bishop*. Jackson: University Press of Mississippi, 1996.

Moore, Marianne. *The Complete Poems*. New York: Macmillan/Viking, 1981.

Moore, Marianne. *The Complete Prose*. New York: Viking, 1967.

Myron, Martin. *The Blake Book*. London: Tate Publishing, 2007

Nitske, Robert W. *Wilhelm Conrad Rontgen*. Tucson: University of Arizona Press, 1971.

O'Connor, Flannery. *The Cartoons of Flannery O'Connor at Georgia College*. Milledgeville: Georgia College, 2010.

O'Connor, Flannery. *Collected Works*. Edited by Sally Fitzgerald. New York: The Library of America, 1988.

O'Connor, Flannery. *The Complete Stories*. New York: Farrar, Straus & Giroux, 1971.

O'Connor, Flannery. *The Habit of Being*. Edited by Sally Fitzgerald. New York: Random House, 1979.

O'Connor, Flannery. *Mystery and Manners*. Edited by Sally and Robert Fitzgerald. New York: Farrar, Straus & Giroux, 1969.

Oppen, George. *Collected Poems*. New York: New Directions, 1975.

Oppen, George. "Statement of Poetics." *Sagetrieb*, vol. 2 (1984): 25–27.

Phillips, Robert. "The Art of Poetry, no. 30" (interview with Philip Larkin). *Paris Review*, Summer 1982.

Phillips, Carl. *From the Devotions*. St. Paul, MN: Graywolf, 1998.

Plath, Sylvia. *The Collected Poems*. New York: Harper and Row, 1981.

Pound, Ezra. *The Literary Essays of Ezra Pound*. Edited by T. S. Eliot. New York: New Directions, 1954.

Rich, Adrienne. "Mr. Bones, He Lives." *The Nation*, May 25, 1964.

Roethke, Theodore. *The Collected Poems of Theodore Roethke*. New York: Doubleday, 1966.

Sanders, Robert. "'Robofly' Solves Mystery of Insect Flight." www.berkeley.edu/news/media/releases/99legacy/6–15–1999

Schwartz, Lloyd, and Sybil Estess, eds. *Elizabeth Bishop and Her Art*. Ann Arbor: University of Michigan Press, 1983.

Shapiro, Karl. *Collected Poems*. New York: Random House, 1978.

Siegel, R. K., and L. J. West. *Hallucinations: Behavior, Experience and Theory*. New York: John Wiley & Sons, 1975.

Simic, Charles. *Selected Poems, 1963–1983*. New York: George Braziller, 1990.

Sontag, Susan. "An Interview with Susan Sontag" (with Geoffrey Movius). *Boston Review,* June 1975.

Stafford, William. *The Way It Is: New & Selected Poems*. St. Paul, MN: Graywolf, 1998.

Stoutenberg, Adrien. *Land of Superior Mirages: New and Selected Poems*. Baltimore: Johns Hopkins University Press, 1986.

Tate, James. "Introduction." In *The Best American Poetry, 1997*. New York: Scribner, 1997.

Tate, James. *The Lost Pilot*. New Haven, CT: Yale University Press,

Tate, James. *The Oblivion Ha-Ha*. Boston: Little, Brown, 1970.

Tauber, Edward, and Maurice R. Green. *Prelogical Experience*. New York: Basic Books, 1959.

Valentine, Jean. *Break the Glass*. Port Townsend, WA: Copper Canyon, 2010.

Voigt, Ellen Bryant. *The Lotus Flowers*. New York: Norton, 1987.

Walter, Donald H. *Building Your Own Airplane*. Ames: Iowa State University Press, 1995.

Wehr, Wesley. "Elizabeth Bishop: Conversations with and Class Notes." *Antioch Review* 39, no. 3 (Summer 1981).

Welty, Eudora. *One Writer's Beginnings*. Cambridge, MA: Harvard University Press, 1983.

Whitman, Walt. *Leaves of Grass*. New York: Dutton, 1971.

Williams, William Carlos. *Autobiography*. New York: Random House, 1951.

Williams, William Carlos. *The Collected Earlier Poems of William Carlos Williams*. New York: New Directions, 1951

Williams, William Carlos. *The Selected Poems*. New York: New Directions, 1969.

Wilson, Margery. *The Woman You Want to Be: Margery Wilson's Complete Book of Charm*. Philadelphia: Lippincott, 1942.

Wolke, Robert L. *What Einstein Told His Barber*. New York: Random House, 2000.

Wright, James. *The Branch Will Not Break*. Middlebury, CT: Wesleyan University Press, 1963.

Wright, Wilbur and Orville. *The Published Writings of Wilbur and Orville Wright*. Edited by Peter Jakab and Rick Young, Washington, DC: Smithsonian Institution Press, 2000.

Yates, Frances. *The Art of Memory*. Chicago: University of Chicago Press, 1966.

Index